Will That Be Regular or Ethyl?

Growing Up Along Route 66 in 1950s Missouri

DeWayne Landwehr

ARCHWAY PUBLISHING

Archway Publishing books may be ordered through booksellers or by contacting:

Archway Publishing
1663 Liberty Drive
Bloomington, IN 47403
www.archwaypublishing.com
1 (888) 242-5904

ISBN: 978-1-4808-7524-1 (sc)
ISBN: 978-1-4808-7523-4 (e)

Library of Congress Control Number: 2019902831

Print information available on the last page.

Archway Publishing rev. date: 03/12/2019

Contents

Foreword

This is a memoir of my early life growing up in a very small town along the famous Route 66, not far southwest of St. Louis, Missouri. As a memoir, it is a story that I believe to be, in the main, true. However, there are conversations in this story that I was not privy to, and therefore are strictly my fantasy. I have included them here to support the story line, but the reader must keep in mind that they are a figment of my imagination, based on my experiences to be true, or at least plausible, but fictional nonetheless.

A word about names. Aside from my family, most of the names used in this story have been altered, disguised, completely changed, or left out altogether, with very few exceptions. It is not my intention to embarrass anyone mentioned or alluded to in this story. I hope you will enjoy this story as a nostalgic look back in time, mostly humorous, with a little spice and some darkness included for realism.

This story is based mostly on my experiences, but my memory was assisted at times by referring to <u>Landwehr and Allied Families</u>, by Michael A. Landwehr. When I mention temperatures and rainfall, I used data from the National Weather Service records. A few photographs were provided by other family members, and by Janice Peterson Hoff. Several of my high school classmates provided some details I had forgotten. My wife, Gail, and Janice provided valuable assistance in previewing the manuscript, and correcting some errors in my memory. Some references to events around World War II and the Cold War were enhanced with information from Wikipedia.

Introduction

Growing up in the 1950's, along Route 66 just outside of St. Louis, Missouri – could there have been anything better? I certainly found it exciting, and have come to realize just how much that period of my life shaped what I am today. Of course, I was convinced everything had always been just like it was then, and would always remain the same. After all, the totality of my experience was wrapped up in my neighborhood, community, school and church, within my few short years in which everything seemed to be static and timeless. Family figured very large in my experience, but also the people from my church and community all played a part in the experiences that shaped my personality, for good or bad. Fortunately for me, the people I interfaced with the most were good people, teaching me the difference between right and wrong. Those experiences taught me to be kind and considerate. Also fortunately, I believe, I was not sheltered from other people who had morals and experiences different from mine. That taught me to be somewhat cautious, and cynical at times. I am very sure now that the balance is not what I wish it had been, but good enough for me to be a contributor to society rather than a detractor.

This is the story of a boy who grew up in the foothills of the Ozarks, in a very small rural town, but close to the historic metropolis of St. Louis. The geography is rolling hills mixed with steep limestone bluffs, especially along river banks. The geology is mineral rich, hard red clay and limestone. Early industries included mining and processing of coal, iron, lead and other minerals. The most abundant trees are oaks, hickories and eastern red cedar, with lots of maple, ash, walnut and sassafras mixed in. Farms in the area tend mostly to pasture because of the difficulty in raising good crops in the hardscrabble earth, except for those lucky enough to own land in one of the river bottoms. The watershed contains three primary rivers; the Meramec, Bourbeuse, and Big River. All drain into the Mississippi, south of St. Louis.

My paternal grandfather owned a farm in Gerald, where he had raised and sold Percherons (large draft horses) and Spanish Jacks during World War I, and between the wars. He also crossbred the horses and Jacks to produce a rather large, durable and mostly docile mule that was very valuable to the military and farmers for pulling very heavy loads. Consequently, they made great engines for pulling either cannons over battlefields or plows through the tough Missouri clay.

As the automotive industry began to mature, there began to be less use for draft horses and mules. For a while, farmers in the area stuck with their animals, but it was becoming clear to Grandpa Julius that the day of draft animals was drawing to a close. A shrewd businessman, and seeing an opportunity in chicken farming, he began a poultry hatchery that seemed to flourish for a time, and especially as World War II began to heat up. As his sons matured and married, he set up each one with another hatchery and feed store in different towns, mostly in Franklin County. I think my father always felt he had drawn the short straw by being assigned to St. Clair for his operation. Indeed, our town was one of the poorer towns in the county. Be that as it may, my parents moved into town with their first two children, and opened a feed store and hatchery on Main Street some time before 1940.

Regardless of St. Clair's economic situation, I was fortunate to find a wealth of goodness in the people that surrounded and nurtured me through my early years, and into adulthood. Sunday School Teachers, classmates, public education teachers, counselors, and interested neighbors all made deep impressions on me that in most cases only came to my consciousness in adulthood.

This is not so much the story of my life as it is the story of how many kind souls helped me along the way into manhood. Most of the story is true. Some memories may have been distorted by time and a poor memory, but this is the way I remember them, so for me the book is factual.

Most of the names have been altered somewhat lest I inadvertently insult someone, as that is not my intention. Those who lived my early life with me will know who the characters are, and that is alright. That might be part of the fun of reading the story. Along the way, you are going to meet some saints, some sinners and not a few shysters who were part of my life.

In many ways, I am convinced that I would not have made it to adulthood without my God and the community around me, but at the same time parts of the community put me at risk for not making it. There were times when I was so disrespectful and disruptive that, in today's world I think I would have been expelled or severely censured; maybe put in jail. At other times, I took physical risks that should have resulted in some type of debilitating injury or death. In many of those instances I was just lucky. In many others though, I can see now that a caring community was watching me, and helping to keep me from harm. I wish that I could write about this great kid who grew into a stellar, bigger-than-life, very successful adult with unquestioned integrity and wealth. That is not me though. I was just another kid from a lower middleclass neighborhood, who somehow made it to adulthood the best he could, and continues in life as best he can, warts and all.

Moving to Town

"**J**ul, Alean and I have been talking it over, and we think it's time to make the move into the hatchery business."

Floyd's father's name was Julius. Although he was very formal in many ways, as most German people are, he allowed friends to call him Jul. As his children became adults and had families of their own, he preferred that they call him by that same familiar abbreviation of his full name. It seemed to be indicative of the almost arm's length relationship he insisted on in most aspects of his family connections.

"So, you've finally realized you can't make it on your own on the farm, eh? Alean's not helping you much either, is she? I told you you should have married better."

Floyd frowned at the insult to his wife and said, "I am not here to discuss Alean with you, and you know damn well that nobody is doing very well this year because of the drought. You've lost several mules, and your crops have burned up too."

"Okay, let's talk business. I have a good place in mind for you in St. Clair, that —"

"Wait, Jul. What about Union?"

"I've already promised Union to Elmer. He lives there already, and he has started planning to build there."

"How about Washington, then? It's prosperous, and would be a good location."

Jul stared him down and said, "I want to have a store on Highway 66, and St. Clair is close to St. Louis, so you'll have better access to a large market. Besides, Washington is a Catholic town, and I don't trust 'em. Everything goes to the pope."

The discussion proceeded into the afternoon, but it finally became apparent that the new store would be in St. Clair, or not at all.

"Okay," Floyd finally said, "When do we start moving?"

"You'll have to stay on the farm through the winter to finish things up there. Besides, winter is a terrible time to open a hatchery. You'll want to open in the spring, when the farmers will have eggs to bring to you. I already have the property picked out, and I'll stake you for the first year. You can start paying me back in the second year."

The hot, dry summer was followed by one of the cruelest winters in memory, with bitter cold winds that blew in heavy snows and stayed for weeks at a time. The cattle would have to be butchered while they still had some meat on them. There was nothing to feed them during the fall and winter. Floyd notified August, the neighborhood butcher, who drove the cows to his farm where they were slaughtered. The beef was sent to St. Louis, and provided some cash that was used to buy blackstrap molasses which Floyd poured, sparingly, over the dry corn fodder. That provided some nourishment for the two remaining cows, which continued to provide a small amount of milk through the winter.

Finally, spring began to make itself known. The cows and chickens were long gone now. The hogs that had made it through the winter were rounded up and sent to market to supply extra cash to be used in stocking the feed store, and to buy eggs for the hatchery. The hatchery was located on Main Street, very near the intersection with Springfield Road. Floyd found a small but comfortable bungalow just a few blocks away from the new store on Main Street, so he would have an easy walk to the store. The little house had only two bedrooms, but there were only three children, and they could make do. Floyd and Alean slept in the main bedroom along with Janet, who was still very small. Jerry was put into the second bedroom, and Maxine slept on a couch.

It was a little scary starting a new business in the middle of the worst depression in American history, but how much worse could it be than what they had been enduring the last several years on a farm that could not produce enough food to live on with the droughts and heat that had plagued everyone? Besides, Floyd was no stranger to hard labor; he was convinced that if he did fail, it would not be for lack of effort on his part. And, in spite of what Julius thought of Alean, she was a hard-working partner for him.

World events were also moving in a direction that gave the fledgling business a boost. There was this madman in Germany who seemed to be moving the world steadily toward another war. Hitler had annexed Austria and invaded Czechoslovakia, and showed no letup in his appetite for more conquests. Although an Englishman named Chamberlain said there now would be "-peace in our time-", the German community in Missouri was skeptical. Most of them had fled to America just a generation or two before to escape the unrelenting militarism of the Kaiser, and knew that Hitler would not keep his word. He would continue to cause trouble in Europe. To make matters worse for the German community, many Americans still harbored deep suspicions and hatred for anything German because of the experience of the First World War.

The anti-German prejudice caused the German immigrant community to close ranks even further, and they were in some respects isolated. Many families spoke German at home, and the church services were in German. Many children at that time could not speak English until they went to public school.

Farmers were seeing an increasing market for eggs and chicken, which meant a better market for a hatchery. Franklin Roosevelt was already sending food and other materials to the British and it looked as though that activity would only grow, not diminish. On September 1, 1939, Hitler invaded Poland, and Britain declared war on Germany. The fat was in the fire now. Britain begged for more help from the US, and Roosevelt responded with the Lend-Lease Act. Food, blankets, oil, coal, ammunition, guns, trucks and everything else needed to survive and wage war were shipped across the Atlantic in great convoys.

Roosevelt knew that America needed to be in the war actively assisting Britain in its attempt to beat the Austrian corporal, but he also knew that Congress and the public would not support entrance into a war that continued to be waged "over there." America continued to sit it out as Holland, Belgium, France, and then Norway were quickly defeated.

There was a temporary scare as it appeared that Hitler had cornered most of the British army on a tiny spit of land on the coast of France at a town called Dunkirk. However, Hitler inexplicably hesitated to deal the death blow, and nearly the entire force was evacuated across the channel in the nick of time using everything that would float.

Finally the Japanese did Roosevelt a great favor by attacking Pearl Harbor on December 7, 1941. Roosevelt's famous "Day of Infamy" speech sealed it; the United States was at war with Japan, and by association, with Germany and Italy.

One of the saddest and more confusing aspects of a state at war is that while some people give their very lives for "the cause", others prosper in the effort to supply their brothers in the conflict. Business was now booming. Every farmer who did not have a chicken coop already was building one and St. Clair Hatchery was selling as many chicks, eggs and feed as Floyd could cram through the tiny store on Main Street. The work involved in running a feed store and hatchery was not as physically demanding as the farm work he had just left, but the hours were about the same - if not longer. Sixteen- to eighteen-hour days seemed to be the norm instead of the exception.

As the war dragged on the food situation worsened. A large part of Europe was in a state of near famine, as battles raged over thousands of square miles. The uncertainty of being able to harvest a crop made planting and long-range planning seem hopeless. The need for foodstuffs from North America, Australia and other regions not overrun by war grew exponentially. Here at home everything was rationed. The purchase of eggs, chicken, beef, pork, gasoline, tires, oil, flour, wheat, and almost everything else was severely restricted. One could not purchase any critical item without the appropriate number of ration stamps.

As a provider of critical war-related goods, Floyd was allotted extra stamps for gasoline and tires, which allowed him to keep his truck running and deliver his products to stores, farmers and the government. However, the tiny size of the store on Main Street severely restricted the volume of goods that could be pushed through it. Something had to be done.

In 1940, a couple of properties became available just a few lots away from the existing hatchery, around the corner on Springfield Avenue, that would allow for plenty of expansion and let Floyd to move his family out of the rental home they had been occupying on Main Street. Floyd was able to buy it for $900. It consisted of about three acres of land and about fifty feet of frontage on Springfield Avenue. This would be the home of the new St. Clair Hatchery. Another small house also became available on Springfield Avenue, just two lots from where the new hatchery would be. Being there would allow Floyd to oversee the construction of the new building, so he rented it and moved the family the few blocks to the new house.

Although the property was now purchased, there was not enough money to build the home and business that would be required so the hatchery stayed at the Main Street location for several more years. In the interim, the war had started for the United States after December 7, 1941, and all unnecessary building activity was severely restricted. Building permits became almost impossible to obtain so the new hatchery building was delayed for several years.

More than that however was the uncertainty of the war's outcome. During the first years of the war, the Allies lost battle after battle and the future seemed anything but assured. Japan had conquered most of the islands leading toward Australia and Hawaii, as well as a large part of Asia, with incursions into China, Burma, and several other small countries in the far east. Italy had made way into Greece, Ethiopia and several countries in North Africa, and Germany had conquered or harassed nearly all of Europe. Nobody was really sure whether the Allies could be victorious, and there was considerable doubt regarding the future of the country. As the allies began to push Japan back to their homeland in the Pacific, however, and successful landings in Africa, Sicily, Italy, and now France indicated there would probably be a satisfactory end to the war, people began to feel more hopeful. Men and women were longing for a return to peace and to be able to live in decent housing – perhaps in their own homes.

As the war began to come to what appeared to be a successful conclusion in 1945, demobilization began to bring the first of several million young men back home, and they all needed a place to live. Since there had been essentially no building for six years there was a tremendous housing shortage.

Because of that shortage, the only way that Floyd could get a building permit was to have the new St. Clair Hatchery designed so that several residential rental units could be included. He also made sure there was plenty of room for a much larger number of incubators for the hatchery. The final design was a rather large sixteen-room brick structure that stood two and a half stories above ground. The basement needed to be somewhat above ground to accommodate a truck ramp to it from the back of the house. That meant that the first floor was about four feet above ground. The ceiling height in the basement was nine feet to accommodate the incubators.

The design was basically that of a shotgun house, with a central hallway that ran from front to back on both floors. On the first floor the feed store was on one side, with family living quarters on the other side. The entire second floor was devoted to residential rentals. There was just one bathroom upstairs though, shared by all tenants, and entered from the hallway.

The war was not over yet, and the demand for Floyd's chickens and eggs was still extremely high. No one could be certain how long the war would last so building began in earnest in 1944. Building materials were in extremely short supply but his business status of being a critical war material supplier helped in Floyd's effort to find and purchase them.

The building project took on extra urgency as 1944 drew to a close. Alean's brother, James, had met and married Annette Kempher on October 11, 1942, just before James had to ship out for the Army to join the war. When he returned at the end of 1944, there was no place for he and his bride to live, so Floyd and Alean took them in. The little two-bedroom cottage was really getting crowded now, with seven people living in it. Additionally, Alean became pregnant with her fourth child – me. Now the new larger house was <u>really</u> a necessity.

With the opening of the St. Clair Hatchery there were now four being operated by the Landwehr brothers, and an article appeared in the St. Clair Chronicle that stated:

"The Landwehrs use a half-million eggs every three weeks and not a single one of them ever goes into the frying pan to become the bosom companion of that famous combination of ham and eggs.

There's a catch to it, of course. It is not an uncommon thing to find several brothers associated in the same business enterprise. But it is quite unusual to find four of them in the same business but with each operating independently of the other and in four scattered communities.

Floyd Landwehr, owner and operator of the St. Clair Hatchery, disclosed this week that each of his three brothers also is in the hatchery business. Elmer operates the Union Hatchery, Marvin the Pleasant View Hatchery at Gerald, and Burton the Fulton Hatchery at Fulton, Missouri. That's where the 500,000 eggs come in. It takes that many every three weeks to keep the four hatcheries operating."

...And Then There Were Six...

I guess it's natural when you're a kid to think that things have always been the way they are right now. Our house had been nearly completed sometime in 1946, the year after I was born. We must not have moved into it immediately, because I have some vague memories of crawling around the house we lived in before that, just two houses east of us on Springfield Avenue. It was a small four-room cottage, and every room was one step up or down from every other room. That's all I remember of the house, but it must have been getting crowded since I was the fourth child.

DeWayne in jumpsuit made by his mother

*Floyd with DeWayne at about nine months,
before we moved into the hatchery*

Alean holding DeWayne

The new house must have been something to behold as it was being built. Situated directly across the street from the public schoolyard, it contrasted quite a bit from the small cottages on either side of it. This was a real brick house – with eight-inch concrete block forming the inner wall giving an overall wall thickness of twelve inches.

The feed store occupied the left half of the first floor and we lived in the right half. A central hallway ran the length of the house and divided the house in half. The upstairs was laid out the same way, except that the right half was divided into three sleeping rooms and the left half was one apartment, all for rent. One bathroom was shared by all the upstairs tenants.

There was an eighteen-foot-wide concrete ramp that angled from the sidewalk in front of the house up to the feed store door. We had a tiny postage-stamp front yard on the right side. Above the front window and door, and extending across the whole front of the house, there was a large Ful-O-Pep sign (the primary brand of feed Dad sold) painted onto the brick with a baby chick on each end, just emerging from the shell. The sign read, "Ful-O-Pep, Makes 'em Fit, not Fat".

Evidently corrugated roofing material had been placed on top of the concrete while it cured, because it had that kind of wavy surface. The aggregate used in the concrete was Meramec River stone; the same stone as used in most concrete mixes, including road surfaces, in Missouri. The unfortunate thing about Meramec stone is that, because it is river stone, all its surfaces are rounded, making it very slick when wet. More than once I slipped and fell while walking down the wet ramp, usually carrying feed out of the store to a waiting car or truck.

Our driveway went along the left side of the house. This was not really a driveway in the sense of most driveways. It did not lead to a garage entrance – it really formed a pathway to the outbuildings at the back of the house. The driveway was not paved, nor did it have much gravel on it. The heavy Missouri clay soil supported even loaded trucks without much problem even when wet. As one proceeded down the driveway, the first thing encountered would be the door to the coal chute, then at the middle of the house was a short loading dock for the feed store. At the back of the house was another ramp that sloped down into the basement. The driveway then made a right turn around the back yard and went past six buildings used for raising chicks to various stages of maturity.

While the clay driveway supported trucks well enough, the clay moved around a bit when wet. Consequently, a center ridge would form periodically, as heavy tires pushed the clay. At some point, usually once a year, we would have to retrieve a mattock, chop away at the ridge, and put the displaced clay back into the ruts.

The driveway, backyard fence and outbuildings divided the property into four zones that we all recognized as kids. The first, of course, was the house. ("Get back in the house!!"). The second was the fenced-in backyard. Just beyond the backyard, and out to the grouping of out-buildings, was a larger play area, and finally beyond the outbuildings, was the Promised Land – an open field where we usually grazed two cows for milk. Only upon reaching a certain age (undefined) and il-lustrating a certain maturity and responsibility level (also undefined) were we allowed there. The back of that field abutted the St. Louis & San Francisco Railroad tracks, and mother was always concerned about hobos carrying us off.

The third area was where we spent most of our time in the summer. It included an open area large enough for us to play softball when we were younger. We had to play on a slope, but didn't mind that. At the top of that slope was an unused chicken house that we used as our playhouse. It was shaded by a mature hickory tree, which also supported a grand tire swing. The Peterson and Landwehr kids spent most of every day there, pretending we were pioneers and settlers in a new land, setting up housekeeping in the wilderness. Janice and Vernon Peterson, my younger brother David and I spent many wonderful days out there.

In the fall we would pick up bushels of nuts that fell from the huge shagbark. After peeling off the husks, we would carry them to the basement where we would smash the nuts with a hammer on the floor, and pick out the juicy nutmeats. My oldest sister, Maxine would make fudge that she would lace with the hickory nuts, and we would all have a real feast.

The Pot of Gold

Thunderstorms are common in Missouri, and some of them can be really spectacular. The schoolyard across the street from us was a few feet higher than the ground on our side of the street, and our house seemed to be on about the lowest ground for a couple of blocks in either direction, so all the runoff from the three school building roofs, the playground, and about half a mile of street drained into the culvert that then ran under our driveway toward the back of the property. The culvert ended just beyond the bend in the driveway and an open drainage ditch then carried rainwater to the back of our property next to the railroad tracks.

One storm in particular really stuck in my mind. The water coming off the school grounds and across the street toward us was running so fast and deep that it looked like a waterfall coming down the schoolyard steps. Even though the drain pipe was 12-inches in diameter, it could not take up the rain fast enough, so the water was standing in front of our house more than a foot deep. As the rain subsided, I watched with fascination as the water swirled around the drain and continued to lower. I wanted to go out and play in the whirlpool, but Mom wisely kept me inside until the water was no longer filling the pipe. This was 1950. I was only five years old, and could easily have been sucked into the whirling water, mud and debris that was then rocketing into the culvert.

I had watched the afternoon thunderstorm develop and burst upon us from the window of the living room in front of the house. I really wanted to be outside, feeling the refreshing shower of the downpour as it came down in buckets on the streets and yards. Mother had called me in however, and made it very clear I was not to wander outside the house until the rain, and especially the lightning, had stopped. Now it almost had, and there was no more holding me back with the appearance of a beautiful, vivid rainbow. The colors were very distinct, and appeared to have been painted across the clearing sky. I exploded from the house, and began running down the sidewalk in the leftover rain from the thunderstorm.

"Where ya headed?" That was Roy, my best friend in the world. He was sitting on his front porch swing, enjoying the cool air following the thunderstorm. "I'm goin' to see if I can find that pot of gold at the end of the rainbow!" Roy laughed, and said, "Let me know if you find it, and I'll help you carry it home." At five years old I had serious doubts about the existence of pots of gold, but with that eternal hope and enthusiasm of young children I had hope that such things could be real.

Roy, approaching 75, was sitting on his front porch swing after the storm, watching the remaining scud drift away, and listening to the thunder continue to move away toward St. Louis. What had been a series of sharp explosions of noise had now faded into an almost continuous low roar as the storm moved off to the east. The air must have cooled off ten degrees already. Gone were the scorching high temperatures of the early afternoon and the choking humidity that kept one's sweat from evaporating to cool the body. "I feel like I am cookin' in my own gravy," he had said earlier, half to himself.

"What? What are you talking about? We're not having gravy to-night!" Lulu, Roy's wife of 55 years, was cranky most of the time, and today was no different. When she was crabby like this, her four chins shook and vibrated against her enormous chest as she talked. Weighing in at well over 300 pounds, she and her mate made an odd pair. Roy couldn't hold down 125 pounds soaking wet, with boots on. When I had first heard the poem about Jack Sprat and his wife, Roy and Lulu came to my mind immediately.

"I was talking about the heat today. It sure feels nice now that the rain has moved through, doesn't it? And the air. It always smells so fresh after a heavy rain; like a brand-new day at the first of spring."

Lulu was not to be denied her bad mood: "This rain will just bring higher humidity tomorrow, and make it unbearable to work in the garden", she said.

Roy sighed, and decided that perhaps silence would be a better strategy just now. Not that it would be much better later, but now, he just wanted to enjoy the fresh smell and cooler air of the evening. No sense badgering her any more. There was no such thing as winning an argument with her anyway.

As predictable as the sunrise, a voice saturated the neighborhood with fingernails-on-blackboard shrillness. "DeWayne!! Time to come in!" My mom could call hogs in from two counties over, and used her powerful megaphone voice several times a day to keep her brood corralled. During these powerful screams, her voice would cover a couple of octaves, giving them a real 'sooie' intonation.

"He just ran down the block a-ways to see if he could find the end of the rainbow", Roy chuckled. "He'll be back in a minute or two."

"I hope so", Alean said, "it'll be dark pretty soon and I want him inside."

"Poor kid", Roy thought, "she keeps him on a real short leash."

Five houses. That was as far as I was allowed to go. Mom had made that very clear many times, and I didn't dare go over the line. I was just turning around when I heard the unmistakable siren call from home. Oh well, I had found out what I thought to be true, so I really didn't need to go any farther anyway. Pot of gold – what a story. I hadn't really believed it when I heard it, but I also wanted to know something else. Can you really find the end of a rainbow? Nope. Five houses proved it. As I ran along the sidewalk, the rainbow just moved along with me – I never got any closer. Wonder how that works? Better get home before Mom gets really mad.

"Where's that pot of gold?"

"I didn't find it this time."

"Maybe somebody beat you to it", he said. That Roy sure is fun. Always teasing and laughing with me. I just love that man.

The family assembled in front of the hatchery

117 In the Shade

loved to work in the garden. Excitement began to build in March, as Mr. Stahlman brought in his pair of mules every spring to plow and disk the garden. I was always amazed that he would just talk to them like people, calling them by name. I thought people had to yell, "giddyup!" if they wanted an animal to move forward, and "Whoa!", when they wanted it to stop. Not so. He would just lift the reins a little and say, "Jake, walk.", in a conversational tone, and the animals would start moving. At the end of a row, he would just say, almost in a whisper, "gee", or "haw", and the mules would turn right or left. Evidently the phrase, 'stubborn as a mule' didn't apply to those two. They seemed to be very compliant. He would do the Landwehrs', then move right next door and do Roy Henry's. Now Roy had a garden! Where our garden covered about a quarter to a third of an acre, Roy's garden covered almost every inch of ground behind his house all the way to the railroad tracks – about two acres! Of course, everyone in the neighborhood had a garden, but Roy's – now that was a garden.

The Landwehrs planted the usual stuff: tomatoes, green peppers, cucumbers, onions, green beans, sweet corn, two kinds of radishes (white icicles, and the round red ones), head lettuce, leaf lettuce, and lots of cabbages. Dad didn't have to tell me how to plant anything, because I had learned that from Roy. Yeah, it was okay to help in the home garden, but helping Roy was really fun. Roy would tell lots of stories that made both of us laugh as we worked. I suspected that most of them were only partly true, but that was alright – they helped pass the time.

Because we raised lots of chickens we had access to lots of chicken manure. Now, chicken manure is very high in nitrogen, and if put on a garden fresh, it would burn the plants to a crisp. So, we had a manure pile – a dung heap – that we allowed to "age" for a year before spreading the goodies on the garden. Boy, did we have produce! We bought very little from the grocery in those days, except flour, sugar, coffee, etc. There was not much need for us to buy canned green beans, corn, ketchup, tomato paste, tomato juice, whole tomatoes, diced tomatoes, okra, potatoes, turnips, tomato sauce, dill, bread and butter or sweet pickles, or sauerkraut. We made all that. Well, we made most of that. Roy, my buddy next door, raised enough turnips, potatoes and okra to feed a small army, so we 'borrowed' those items.

I usually had to go to Mrs. Wells' house (the fifth house away) to 'borrow' some dill. She seemed to produce all the dill everyone in the neighborhood needed, so we all 'borrowed' from her. I always thought it was odd that Mom would say 'borrow' when it was obvious she was not going to return the dill. The meaning of community sharing had not fully been impressed on me at that point. I think everyone knew the phrase meant recognition of a favor that would be gladly returned when needed or requested.

When the weather was good and the garden responded, we would be flooded with vegetables, and we would can for days as it ripened. When the vegetable canning would slow down, Mom would make jelly and preserves from plums, strawberries, blackberries, grapes and peaches. It was not uncommon for Mom to put up four or five hundred jars of various kinds of things. The canning work was hot, as she would keep the pressure cooker going most of the day. And when she made sauerkraut, man the house would smell. She took care of the cooker and the stove, and cut up most of the vegetables. I filled the jars.

Spring of 1954 had long since passed, and most everyone's garden had looked really great until recently. "Let's stop for a few minutes and get a drink of water", Roy gasped. "You know it's 117 in the shade today? We have to be careful, or we'll get sunstroke." Roy took down the dipper that always hung on the outside corner of his back porch, and drew some water out of the standpipe next to the house. "Here, now don't drink too fast, or you'll get a headache."

"Thanks, Mr. Henry, that really tastes good today. Why did you say it's 117 in the shade? We don't work in the shade, so why do we care what the temperature is there? Why don't you measure it where we work? It's a lot hotter out there, and that's where I want to know how hot it is."

"You know, that's a very good question, and someday I'll bet you'll figure it out", Roy said with another of his signature laughs.

It did get hot that summer. Trees burned up and dropped their leaves, thinning the shade even further. Lawns and gardens dried up. Walking on grass sounded and felt like walking on corn flakes, because it just crinkled and broke off when your foot came down. Nobody had to mow their yard, but there was not much home-grown produce, either. Huge cracks appeared in the ground as the soil dried up. Livestock died in the fields. At the hatchery, chickens died by the hundreds. Some people died, especially in the cities, because very few people had air conditioning. We were awakened one night by an explosion that sounded like a cannon had been fired in our house. All of us ran out of our bedrooms to find green beans all over the dining room walls, ceiling, and floor. Mom had bought a few cans of green beans at the store to supplement what we had produced. She had stored them in the pantry cupboard between the dining room and kitchen. One of them had blown up in the cupboard and ruptured a couple more stacked next to it, blowing the door of the cupboard open in the process and spraying everything with green beans.

Floyd worked his way through the battery house filled with cages of growing chicks. It was called the battery house because it was filled with these cages which were called batteries. Each one was a vertical stack of six cages about 36 inches square and ten inches high. Each cage had feed and watering troughs that hung on the outside and a heated area in the back that was curtained off from the feeding area in the front. Up to 100 newly-hatched chicks could be put in each cage and raised for a few weeks for those customers who wanted to buy their chicks already "started" a few weeks before they took delivery of them. That saved them from having to purchase heat lamps and the equipment required to care for flocks of small chicks.

Today was another in a string of unpleasant days in which Floyd had to reach into each cage and pull out the dead and dying chicks that had succumbed to the heat. At first, it was just one or two each day, but now he went through the building with a bucket that was filled with dead birds by the time he had finished. *"How long is this heat going to last"*, he asked himself. It had started getting unusually warm by the middle of June. Beginning June 10, the high temperature was over 90 every day through July. In those six weeks, there were fifty-two days over 90. June 25 started a streak of four weeks where the daily high temperature was near or over 100^0 every day. During that streak, on July 14, 1954, the temperature reached 118^0, the highest temperature ever recorded in Missouri for any day. The hellish hot streak ended Labor Day weekend, after 89 days of suffering for everyone. Out of those 89 days, there were only seven days below 90, and 32 - more than one out of three - above 100 degrees.[1]

As he continued through the battery house, his clothes became saturated with his own sweat. The heat was made all the worse because of the infamous Missouri summer humidity. Sweat didn't evaporate and cool him; it just sat on the skin and made him feel miserable. His

---

[1] National Weather Service. Rolla, Missouri, weather station

hatband was soaked and sweat rolled out from under it like a waterfall to drip from his eyebrows, nose and chin onto the floor. His heavy, blue cotton work pants looked as if someone had poured a bucket of water in his lap, as he was soaked from the waistband down to his knees. *"If this continues much longer, I won't have any chickens to sell at all."*

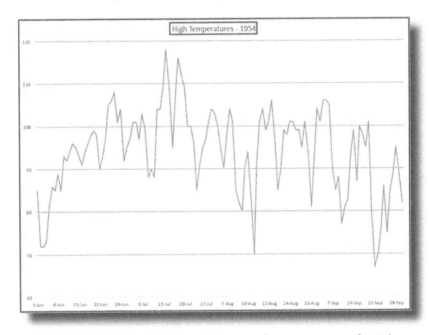

High Temperatures in central Missouri during summer of 1954

He was becoming light-headed, and recognized the signs of heat prostration creeping up on him. He stopped for a drink of water from the standpipe and thought of a similar time, almost exactly twenty years before. It had seemed so long ago just this morning, but now, in his heat-induced near-delirium, he could see it clearly as if he were there again. He stood there, looking out the window, but did not see what was in front of him. Instead, he saw himself as a young man standing in the open door of the new barn he had just built, looking at the beautiful bottom land full of corn he had planted in that spring of 1934. In June, the corn nearly leaped from the ground, looking full and deep green. It was going to be a great year, with a good crop and plentiful pasture for his small herd of dairy cows and pigs.

Now it was the end of July. The corn had tassled out beautifully, and the seed was beginning to swell on the ears. Then, a savage wind from Hell blew in at mid-month, and brought with it temperatures well over 100°, that lasted until mid-August. From July 14 to August 8, six record temperatures were set, at or near 110°.[2] What had been the beginnings of a bountiful harvest turned into a field of black, withered stalks that bore no fruit at all. The corn leaves rattled in the wind so loudly you could hear them at the house, more than one hundred yards away. Grass in the yard crackled and disintegrated under foot, blowing away on the Dantesque wind, leaving bare ground that was pounded and spun into dust devils that danced across the farm.

There would be no corn crop. To make matters worse, there was no pasture. His six cows had lived on the dried grass until August, but then that was all gone. They stopped giving milk, and became very thin. If they were to be saved, some forage had to be found. There was no hay to buy, and he could not have afforded it if there had been. Normally, supplemental hay was not required until at least December, and cattle could usually be turned into the harvested corn fields to forage for dropped corn and corn stubble. But here it was August, and there was no corn crop, no pasture, and no hay available.

The only solution was to harvest the corn as fodder. From then until the next spring, the poor cows were kept alive with the dried fodder, laced with a little blackstrap molasses. By then, they were emaciated skeletons, just carrying their hides around. The pigs had to be slaughtered early and smoked. There was no point taking them to market. Every farmer was having to do the same thing. Beef and pork had flooded the markets, and were worth almost nothing. Many animals were just slaughtered and buried.

As with many farmers at that time, the horrible weather conditions hastened his decision to leave the farm. It was a very tough decision. This

---

[2] National Weather Service.

was the home place. Three generations of Landwehrs had already farmed this land, and it felt like leaving for a new world.

Now, as he stared unseeing out the window, he reflected on the current situation. This year could bankrupt him. How did this happen? Just a few short years ago, he owned a business deemed critical to the war effort, and was making a handsome living providing food for the Allied troops. Now, he was just barely hanging on again, brought low by this damnable weather. He roused himself from his self-pitying stupor and looked out the door. There was DeWayne, sharing a drink with Roy Henry. Everybody needed water today.

With five kids in the family, and just three bedrooms to work with, Mom and Dad had decided to expand and change things around a bit. Until then, our parents had slept in the front bedroom, next to the kitchen, with David, who was still in a crib. Jerry (the oldest) and I slept in the room immediately behind that room in bunk beds, and my two older sisters, Maxine and Janet, slept in the back room across the hall, directly behind the feed store. Jerry was now a teenager, and needed a room by himself, so Dad built a staircase from the hallway up to the second floor, and into what had been one of the sleeping rooms upstairs. (It was now several years since the end of the war, and the housing shortage had eased substantially. Consequently, there was less demand for the sleeping rooms that had been so critical earlier.) I was moved into the front bedroom, and Mom and Dad moved into the back bedroom with David, who was just a toddler.

I wasn't totally thrilled with the move, because now I was by myself. Sure, I had gone from a bunk bed to a double, but I had actually liked the bunk bed. Besides, I looked up to Jerry and was disappointed that we had been separated. Jerry seemed to always be in trouble, and it had actually been kind of fun to watch Dad come into our bedroom on many occasions to lecture him for some transgression. Not that I really hoped for Jerry to get into trouble; it was just nice for someone else to be in the barrel instead of me for a change.

One nice thing to come out of that move was that I had moved into a much cooler room. My bed was now against the wall, and I found that by wedging myself between the wall and the bed, I was much cooler.

The room was on the east side of the house and shaded by a gigantic maple tree, but more than that, the house was a real brick house, with twelve-inch thick walls. On really hot nights it felt so good to get wedged against the wall and be cooled by the concrete block inner wall surface.

On warm nights after I had put on my pajamas, I would sometimes sit in the front yard and enjoy the cool night air. If I happened to get out there at dusk, I could watch the chimney swifts return for the night. The school buildings across the street were heated by coal-fired boilers that were housed in the middle building, and it sported a gigantic brick chimney that seemed to reach the sky. Every evening, especially in late spring and summer, the sky would be turned almost black by the thousands of swifts returning to roost in the chimney. The mass of birds looked like a whirling tornado descending into it. I often wondered how they lived in the chimney when the heat was turned on in the winter. I wasn't aware then of the fact that they migrate.

Another of my "friends" in those front yard visits was an enormous toad that lived in the flower bed next to the porch. The first time I saw him and picked him up, he employed his self-defense mechanism and peed on my hand. He tried to jump away from me, but I held on to him. I stroked his head and back a few times and put him back to the ground gently. After a few more evening encounters like that, he got used to me, and would let me pick him up and stroke his back. Then I looked for him every time I went out. Sometimes, I would just go out to find him, then would come back into the house. It was like having my own secret pet.

One summer evening as I sat on the metal lawn chair in the front yard I noticed two people on the playground across the street at the school. I recognized them, but didn't know their names; they were a few years older than me. They obviously thought the darkness of the night hid them from view, but I could see them very well, as my night vision improved. He had pulled his jeans down to his knees and sat on the swing. She had hiked her dress up and sat on his lap, facing him. There was quite a bit of giggling and moaning going on, and it wasn't long before I figured out what was happening. It was interesting, but I wasn't quite into that yet. I doubt if they saw me, because I was also sitting in the dark, with the house at my back, not highlighted by the moon.

Hijinks and Critters

Jerry was the oldest in the family, and had been born on 'the home place' in Strain. In keeping with family tradition, his middle name, Floyd, was his father's first name. Floyd had likewise been named Floyd Julius, with his father's first name as his middle name. Jerry was always into animals, and there was never a dull moment when he and his best buddy Dee got together. Dee Henry lived just a few houses down the street to the east, and was at our house nearly every day. He and Jerry were always scheming and getting into some kind of trouble.

We were all asleep in bed one night, and a terrible scream from somewhere woke all of us up. Mom went into hysterics.

"Floyd, wake up! It sounds like someone is being killed, and I think it is coming from the basement!"

Actually, Mom didn't have to wake him, or anybody else in the house for that matter, because the sound was very loud and terrifying. We all followed Dad into the basement, except Jerry, who was asleep on the second floor, and wasn't at all surprised by the sound.

In the basement, in a wire cage normally used for chickens, was a tiny screech owl, who thought it was time to wake up and go hunting. I wondered how such a little creature could produce such a God-awful racket, but there it was.

"Jerry, get down here right now!!" Mom could out-screech even a screech owl.

Jerry came scurrying down to the basement in his briefs and wife-beater undershirt (we didn't sleep in pajamas). The rest of us were standing around the cage in our pajamas or underwear, except Dad, who was wearing his usual long johns. We all stared at Jerry – who else would have brought a wild creature into the house?

"Where did this come from?!"

"Dee and I caught it a few days ago, and I brought it home."

"Just what did you intend to do with it?"

"I thought I might raise it."

"Oh, no you won't. Get it out of here right now."

Dad nodded his head toward the back door and said, a lot more quietly, "Let it go, Jerry. Now." I think Dad was more upset about having to come downstairs and deal with this than the fact that Jerry had the bird, but we all marched to the saying that, 'if mama ain't happy, ain't nobody happy.'

Jerry grumbled something under his breath, hung his head, and dutifully picked up the cage and carried it out into the night. He opened the door on the top of the cage, left it sit there, and came back inside. The poor little owl didn't move for a few seconds, and then suddenly took flight and left us in (almost) quiet.

Mom said, "Now, everybody get back to bed. And Jerry, stop bringing all these animals home!"

"Ah, Mom!" He moped back up to his room, and the rest of us went to bed. I had thought the whole thing was pretty exciting, and I wasn't the one in trouble for once. What a great night!

Mom did have a point. Jerry already had a cage in the back yard with about fifty turtles in it, and an aviary with a couple hundred pigeons. I'm not sure what he intended to do with either of those collections, but they were fun to have, I guess. At various times, he also experimented with chinchillas, pheasants, quail, and other animals.

Sometime after that, Jerry came into the house as proud as he could be, and said he had another animal to show us, but he hadn't brought it into the house this time. He had it in a cage out back, and wanted us all to come and look at it. Since it was after dark he had a flashlight, and we all tromped out to see what he had this time. We walked down the driveway at the side of the house, and to the back of the property where some spare batteries (chicken cages) were sitting outside. He stopped and waited for us all to assemble around the cage, and turned the flashlight into the cage. There was an adult skunk, looking right at us, and decidedly unhappy. Its back end was raised, and its tail was pointed toward us, over its head. You couldn't have blown us apart any quicker with dynamite. We scattered to the four winds, everyone screaming.

As you can imagine, that find wasn't very popular with the family, either. I have no idea how he had managed to corral that skunk, bring it home, and get it into the cage without being sprayed, but he did. Mom was not pleased. He had to get rid of that too.

The hatchery business was not doing well after the end of WWII, so Dad had a lot of spare equipment. There were several of the batteries that had been moved outside and were sitting around the back of the lot. Jerry found a great use for them. He and Dee decided there was money to be made in Angora rabbits. The plan was to raise these rabbits, butcher them and sell the meat to grocery stores and the hides to fur apparel manufacturers. I think the idea had been promoted by people who sell Angora rabbits.

There were just a couple of problems with this plan. They really didn't confirm the market demand. It turns out that not that many people like eating rabbit. And, at least in our part of the country, those who do, enjoy hunting their own. They don't go to the store looking for it. Next, there was the issue of curing and tanning the hides. That's a lot of hard, smelly work that involves equipment and some kind of nasty chemicals if you're going to do more than a few of them. Perhaps the most glaring oversight though, was the problem of inventory control. Once they had bought their first breeding pair, they were off to the races, and couldn't bring themselves to separate them. Before long, the entire back yard was full of cages with lusty rabbits and bunnies. They were everywhere. At some point, they decided the enterprise was useless, but I don't know how they got rid of all those rabbits. They must have had close to 500 before they stopped the production line.

He also tried some experiments with chinchillas, quail, pheasants and maybe a few other species before giving up on that idea. Then he and Dee decided they could probably sell knick-knacks made of plywood. Dee's father Grover had a shop full of great woodworking tools, and the boys decided to 'borrow' those tools for their latest project. They carted jigsaws, drill presses, clamps, vises, and various other tools from Dee's house to ours and reinstalled them all in our basement. Grover was not too happy, because as it turned out, he hadn't been consulted about this loan of his prized tools. He allowed the conspiracy to continue however, and the two started their business with some interesting shelves that they hawked to the neighbors and townsfolks. After a while they even sold some of them to a souvenir shop along Route 66.

When you raise as many chickens as we did, in confined spaces especially, you cannot avoid the problem of mites, lice and sundry other unpleasant critters. I can recall several occasions when I returned to the house after cleaning out one of the chicken houses and discovering large numbers of mites all over my body upon removing my clothes for a bath. Therefore, it was common for us to fumigate the areas periodically. The process involved emptying the building of all living creatures you wanted to save, and closing all openings, such as windows, doors and any vents. Then the fumigation liquid was mixed and poured into a little can that was heated electrically. The heat slowly boiled off the liquid and the resulting gas killed the unwanted critters. After 24 hours, the building was opened up and allowed to air out before repopulating it. The fumigant had a very unmistakable, pungent, unpleasant odor, so it was not likely that anyone would inadvertently walk into a space being fumigated.

Mrs. Hibbard, the school principal, was always at her office very early. She usually made it a practice to walk the halls before everyone arrived, just as a way to ensure that everything was ready for the students and teachers. This particular morning, she sensed something was not quite right as she unlocked the door, walked through the outer office, unlocked the door to her inner office and hung her coat in the closet. Something was in the air.

As she walked back into the hall, she was positive; there was definitely something wrong. The farther she walked, the worse the smell. Now she was beginning to get nauseous and light-headed. The smell was getting stronger. Something must be wrong in the science classroom. Maybe some chemical spill. What a mess that could be. She opened the door into the science room, and yes, the smell was there, but not any stronger than in the hall. She looked around the workbenches, in the cupboards where the chemicals were kept, and in the storage areas under the counters. Nothing was out of the ordinary.

The National Guard occupied some offices in the lower level. Maybe they had been doing something with chemical weapons. She walked over to their office door, and sniffed. No, the smell was not any worse here, but it was generally getting worse all over. She now held her handkerchief up to her nose as she walked. Because this was a military space, she didn't have a key to enter, so she walked, hurriedly now, back to her office and telephoned the commander of the national guard unit at home.

"Hello, this is Mrs. Hibbard at the school. Has the National Guard been doing any experiments, or any other work, with chemicals, chemical weapons, or anything that might smell bad?"

"No, Ma'am, we are not a chemical weapons unit, and we have nothing like that in our possession."

"Well, there is definitely something wrong here, and since I cannot access your area, I need for you to get over here right away, and make sure there is nothing wrong in there. And, while you're here, you might be able to help us find out what and where this awful smell is coming from, if not from your area."

"Sure, Mrs. Hibbard. I'll call a couple of people, and we'll help you police the area."

So, the National Guard was called out.

The smell was getting worse by the minute, and Mrs. Hibbard was feeling faint. She went back to her office, and retrieved a scarf to hold over her nose, along with her handkerchief, then continued her search. Teachers began arriving, and as they did, each one would come running to find her with the awful news that there was a terrible stench in the building.

Now, some of the students began to arrive and complain about the awful odor. Fortunately, most of them tended to play out on the playground first, instead of coming right into the building.

Okay, now it was getting unbearable. She hurried to the closest classroom and yelled through the door, "Throw open all the windows! Go and tell all the other teachers. Open all the windows."

So, on a fairly cold fall day, with the radiators all calling for heat, causing the steam boilers to crank into high gear, all of the building walls were perforated by open windows, which caused the radiators to call for more heat.

The noxious fumes continued to get worse. She had to do something drastic. The National Guard had scoured their area and determined that there was nothing amiss in their area. Then they had joined the effort to open all windows, and at the same time to search every room for something – anything – that might be causing this catastrophe.

All the students were told to stay outside. Teachers were beginning to get sick. The National Guard had found nothing. She had found nothing. The teachers had found nothing. The smell was getting worse. There was only one thing to do. School had to be cancelled. Teachers were told to inform the students to go home; there would be no school today. Hopefully, the source of this awful plague would be found today, and school could be resumed tomorrow. Fortunately at this time there was no bussing, and all the students were local, so it was just a matter for the children to walk home. Most mothers would be home to receive them.

After the students had been sent home and nearly everyone had left, a student came forward with some information.

"Good morning, Mr. Landwehr?"

"Hello, yes, this is Floyd. What can I do for you, Mrs. Hibbard? Are you having a fire drill this morning? I see all the kids out on the playground and around the school."

"No, apparently someone has put fumigant behind a lot of the radiators, and we have had to dismiss school for the day. I suspect the fumigant might have originated from your store. Might you know anything about that?"

"No, I don't, but you're right; we do use and sell fumigant. It could have come from here, or it might have come from the MFA store downtown. Have you checked there?"

"Well, actually, I have already questioned Jerry and he has confessed to the prank. I really called you as a courtesy to let you know we are going to have to suspend Jerry for this. It is very serious you know. Some students and faculty may become ill because of this, and we have had to close the school for the day, which is a very expensive proposition."

"Thank you, Mrs. Hibbard. Jerry will also be paying a steep price when he gets home."

As anyone could have guessed, Jerry was not alone in this caper. Dee was right there as a co-conspirator, as was another friend of his. I don't know who did the planning, but they all participated. Jerry and Dee were suspended for five days. Jerry was punished although I really think Dad was as much amused as angry about the whole thing.

Good Morning, Class

A t that time in our school system, there was no pre-school or kindergarten. Education began with the first grade. The three school buildings across the street from our house were evenly divided. The first, and largest, building, was for grades one through four. The second, somewhat smaller building was for grades five through eight, and the third, and considerably smaller building was for the high school – grades nine through twelve. All the buildings were brick, three-story affairs. The first two buildings were also connected with an underground tunnel, which was used as a tornado shelter. The school cafeteria was in the basement of the second building, so the elementary students took the tunnel to the cafeteria every day.

In the elementary grades, we stayed in one classroom for all our classes. Toward the end of fourth grade, conversations turned to the more 'grown-up' task of switching rooms for our various classes. Not that we were scared; we were just mindful that this required some additional thought on our part, so we didn't get lost. Jerry's class approached this new responsibility with its typical irresponsibility.

"Good morning, boys; hello girls!"

"Good morning, Mr. Jacobs."

Mr. Jacobs was standing against the open door to his classroom, in the hallway, greeting all the new incoming students as they entered his classroom.

"What pleasant kids,", he was thinking, as the students filed into his classroom. "Maybe this won't be as difficult as I thought. Perhaps the reputation of this class has been exaggerated."

The teachers had discussed this particular class at length, because of their apparent bent toward mischief. Their first five years had been marked by several suspensions, and a couple of expulsions. But here they were, looking bright, being friendly, and seemingly orderly, as they greeted him respectfully and filed into the room in orderly fashion.

"Good morning, Mr. Jacobs!"

"Good morning Jerry, Hello Dee. Glad to see you this morning."

Wait...Hadn't they already come through the door earlier? He turned to his right to look into the classroom. The first thing he noticed was that there were very few children in there. The next thing he noticed was that most of the kids were jumping out the window. Then they were running back around to the front and entering again. Although this class was on the first of the three floors, there was still a six or seven-foot drop to the ground. They could get hurt! He ran to the windows and shut them with a bang, and stood glaring at the class, just as Jerry and Dee approached the door again.

"Don't even bother coming in again, boys. Just go ahead to Mrs. Hibbard's office. I think you both know the way by now."

"(Sigh)...I was too quick and optimistic, wasn't I?", Mr. Jacobs thought to himself, as he turned to address the rest of the class. Most of them were also in on this prank, and he had to re-establish control or lose the class completely. Dee and Jerry, in the meantime, strolled to Mrs. Hibbard's office, laughing until they got close. Then they switched to appropriately contrite expressions, secure in the knowledge that there would be some punishment, but they had successfully been able to skip another class.

And so it went, through and into high school and beyond, for many in the class. A few ended up in trouble with the law.

Softball

There were really only three sports in our small school system: basketball, track, and softball. Jerry played first base on the high school softball team. His best buddy Dee was the catcher, and another really good friend was the pitcher. Until the middle '50s, there was really no bus service for the school. The teams were hauled around to other schools in parents' and coaches' cars. At that time, Dad had a small panel truck for the business. Three people could sit on the bench seat in front, but the center position was somewhat problematic because of the floor mounted gear shifter. The back was completely open. It was constructed with vertical gussets welded to the sheet metal. It also had wooden slats that ran front to back, and bolted to the gussets. For purposes of hauling the team around, Dad had cut a couple of 2 x 10 boards that extended across the width of the back. The ends of those boards rested on the wooden slats. Four guys could sit on each of those slats, so we could easily haul eight of the players. I don't remember if we actually squeezed nine into the truck or not. Mom would sit in the front passenger seat, and I sat on her lap.

After high school the team wanted to stay together, and St. Clair had a city softball league, divided into Junior and Senior brackets. There were roughly ten teams in each bracket, which made for about 200 people participating directly on the teams. That was a pretty hefty percentage in a town with only 2,400 total population. Jerry and Dee persuaded Dad to sponsor a team, so they entered the Junior bracket. Dad also served as the team manager, head coach, owner and chief deep pocket. This gesture proved to be very valuable to the players, but also to the community. The players had little desire to be absorbed into the other teams in the league, but wanted to continue relating to each other. This team gave them a way to accomplish that, and it kept them out of mischief for the most part. Since Dad's business was St. Clair Hatchery, that was the name on the team T-shirts. And, since, Dad had six kids at the time, he took a lot of ribbing about hatching his own team. (Jane had come along in 1951 as the youngest sibling.)

As much as we like to look at the past through rose-colored glasses and imagine that things and people were great, if we are honest we have to admit that people are pretty much the same through time. Oh sure, some things change, but there have always been good and bad players on the scene. More than a few of the kids Jerry's age had their share of troubles with the law and society in general. Dad's willingness to work with those kids, and offer his time to coach them and haul them around the county to games was a godsend to many who were "at risk", and there were some.

Joe was the pitcher on our softball team. I say 'our team'; I was too young to play, but attended every game, so felt a strong sense of ownership. Joe was tall and slender, and moved like pond water. He did not stand erect, but walked sort of stoop-shouldered and scuffed his feet, as if he hardly had the energy to make it to the pitcher's mound. When Joe spoke, it was as if there were molasses coating every word, slowing them down as they came out of his mouth. You didn't want to be in a hurry if you were talking to Joe, because you would soon be wanting to reach in and pull out every thought; otherwise you might succumb to old age before he could finish a sentence.

Batters who faced him for the first time were always taken by surprise by his first few pitches, because they were blisteringly fast. As Joe started his windup, one had the impression that he might fall asleep before delivering the pitch, but then his arm came down, and the next thing the batter knew was that there was a very loud POP! as the ball hit the pocket of the catcher's mitt. His rocket-like fastball combined with very impressive curves, drops and changeups made for a formidable arsenal. After facing a few of his fastballs, I saw one person swing twice at the same pitch, his changeup, missing it both times. It seemed to defy gravity as it floated to the plate and once there, ended with a near-vertical drop to the dirt.

Dee Henry, Jerry's best friend, was the catcher. He was medium height and slender, but tough as nails. He never ran from a fight, and that would get him into trouble later on, but his scrappy nature stood him in good stead as catcher. On close plays at the plate, he was fearless in blocking the plate.

On one occasion an opposing player, built like a tank, had hit a long ball to left field and was determined to make it a home run. Greg fielded the ball on the first bounce and could see that he had a play at the plate, so he launched it directly to the plate instead of to Odie, the cutoff man at shortstop. Dee was waiting for it and stood blocking the plate with the ball in hand as the runner rounded third base. The logical thing for the runner to do was to hold up and return to third base, but he was determined that Dee was not going to stop him. He came barreling into Dee, obviously not caring that he would be out, or perhaps thinking that he could jar the ball out of Dee's hand, because he didn't attempt to slide or otherwise avoid a collision. He smashed into Dee, leading with his elbow, and drove them both to the ground. I think Dee ended up with three cracked ribs, but the runner was out.

Years later, Johnny Cash sang about "A Boy Named Sue", and when I heard it I often thought of this softball team. Among the starters' names, we had a Sharon, Dee, and a couple others that could be girls' names. You didn't want to mess with any of them.

The ball diamond was on the school grounds, and the gymnasium stuck just barely out of fair territory, way out in right field. The roof of the gymnasium was roughly two and a half stories high. Sharon batted left handed, and put more softballs onto that roof than any other player I ever saw, on any team. If the ball sailed over first base in fair territory then curved just a little, it would be an unreachable home run.

Greg batted right handed and was probably the second highest home run hitter on the team, after Sharon. The ball diamond was typical of most small-town ball diamonds, with the announcer's hut perched behind home plate above the concession stand. However, our field had no outfield fence, so there was no such thing as a ball hit 'out of the park', unless you managed to hit that sliver of roof off of right field, as Sharon often did. If you hit the ball anyplace else, there was no coasting to the plate. You beat feet all the way.

Greg played left field, and was outstanding as a fielder as well as being a strong hitter. One of the skills a player must have to be a good outfielder is the ability to turn his back on the plate and charge after long fly balls while looking over his shoulder for the ball's flight path. Greg was doing just that one night and ran full tilt into the last light pole, hitting it nearly dead center. He bounced back several feet and lay, unmoving, on his back and spread-eagle. We rushed him across the street to our home and looked him over. By the time we got him home, he had a purplish knot on his forehead the size of the softball he had been chasing. I remember hearing the word 'concussion' for the first time, and don't remember if he played the rest of the game, but I remember him saying he wanted to.

Speaking of the announcer's hut, ours was constructed in the conventional manner with large windows on three sides. Those windows served as the serving counters during games, and had shutters hinged at the top that could be hooked from the inside to lock them up. Vernon and I discovered that they were locked with large hooks at the very bottom of the shutters, and not very tightly at that. It was easy for us to get our small hands between the shutter and the frame, and scoot the hook out of the eye. It was then a simple matter of climbing over the counter and squeezing under the shutter. After doing our "breaking and entering", we explored the interior, which was pretty small. I don't know why we wanted to get in there; we were just exploring, I think. The old cash register was sitting there on the counter, so we opened it and found a treasure trove – two pennies! Our first bank robbery. I think I was seven.

After a few years of consistently winning the Junior bracket, the team was moved to the Senior bracket. The team continued to have fun together, but the league was faltering. Little League (Khoury League) baseball had come to town, and attendance at the softball games fell off to just a few diehard fans. The game had evolved for everyone from a serious competition to just some evening fun.

One evening we were designated the visiting team, so we had the third base bench. It was late in the game, and it had turned into quite a route, with our team running away with the score. Dee was coaching third base, and there was one runner on base. Someone hit a long line drive into deep center field (remember, there is no fence), and the outfielders were chasing the ball as it seemed to roll forever. Dee waved the runner on to home plate, then stepped onto third base and ran home himself. As he did that, someone else had taken his spot as third base coach. He waved the batter in, and then he also stepped onto third base and ran home. The crowd saw what was happening, and roared with laughter, made all the funnier because the score keeper hadn't noticed, and posted four runs!

About this time, a guy I only knew as Pappy approached Dad and wanted to pitch for the team. He had to be at least sixty, and Dad was very dubious about his ability to pitch. He really wanted his son to be able to play on Dad's team, and that was part of the package. If his son didn't play, he didn't either. He didn't want to take our pitcher's place. He said he would only be good for a couple of innings, but almost guaranteed that there would be no hits during those two innings. Dad agreed to take on the pair on a trial basis. So now, we had one pitcher who looked too tired to throw a ball, and another who looked old enough (and may have been) to be grandpa to most of the other players. True to his word, there were almost never any hits when Pappy pitched. He had a blistering fastball, and a wicked curve.

After a couple years consistently winning the Senior bracket, they were 'invited' to split up and divide the players among the other teams. I can still recall the conversation.

Dad had been invited to attend an organizational meeting of the league, as one of the sponsors. He took me along. I must have been around seven or eight. Chairs were arranged in a circle; the sponsors facing each other in hopes of finding a way to bring back the zeal and participation of the past. In their minds, part of the problem was the dominance of the St. Clair Hatchery team, with its youth and exuberance on display at every game. To counter that, Dad opined that many of the kids on his team were on the edge of being in trouble, and that they had no desire to play on another team. The comradery of the team is what brought them together and, in his mind, kept them 'out of the bars and off the streets'. He expressed that if they were split up most of them would quit.

His argument did not win out of course, and the team was split up. As he predicted though, many of them quit playing. He formed a traveling team of the former squad, and they tried to keep it together for awhile, but the death blow had been dealt. The league quickly fell apart and the town lost interest in supporting the sport. Baseball was coming in for the younger kids, in the form of the Khoury League, but the older teens and adults were left out in the cold.

Slim

Joe's younger brother was about my age, and his nickname was Slim. I really don't know where the nickname came from, but that was it. Since neither of us were old enough to play ball, we took the opportunity to try to make some spending money.

Each team had to furnish a new softball to start the game. If both softballs were lost or damaged substantially during the game, they had to furnish more for the game to continue. Since the cost of the balls came out of the team sponsors' pockets, they obviously did not want to lose any of those balls. For that reason, Sharon caused my dad some frustration, because he put more balls out of action than anyone else by putting them on the school roof – but he also produced a lot of runs. Team managers would pay for recovered foul balls, so we stayed alert and chased after them. The going rate was $0.10 for each recovered ball, and we could sometimes return as many as five balls during a game. Of course, the players would recover any that were close to the diamond, but many foul balls went well out of the park.

Another revenue stream for us was discarded soda bottles. The stands were just two-by-twelve boards laid across concrete block risers, and people would merely drop the empty bottles down to the ground. We would crawl under the bleachers and retrieve those bottles, and return them to the concession stand for our reward; a penny each. That doesn't seem like much today, but five of those would buy a bottle of Pepsi.

One summer day Mom asked, "How would you like to stay overnight with Slim at his house?" I answered, "Sure. How long?"

"Oh, a couple of days. Mrs. Jenkins thought it might be good for Slim to have the company of a boy who is well-behaved, and could learn from him."

I thought, *"and that's me??"* but said, "Ok, that would be great."

The Jenkins' house was a three-room cottage set off the gravel county road about 200 feet. The front room had been a porch at one time but had been closed in. It went all the way across the house and served both as a living room and the second bedroom at night. Behind that was the kitchen and eating area, and the main bedroom. There was a small porch in the back on which stood an old Frigidaire icebox that was still in use. There was a shed behind the house that housed a small number of chickens and a goose named Ozzie.

Ozzie was mean and would spread his wings, hiss and charge us whenever we came outside. I soon found out what made Ozzie so mean. Slim would stand his ground, and as the goose approached, he would reach out and smack Ozzie across the head, causing the long neck to swing to the side, and the goose would momentarily lose his balance and stagger. Then Slim would run away and Ozzie would honk violently and chase him. I noticed that Ozzie did not charge Mrs. Jenkins, so it was obvious that Ozzie just feared and/or hated Slim. I guess because I was nearly the same size as Slim, Ozzie put me in the same category as him, and I steered clear of the goose.

Slim also had a cute little terrier named Spot (very original, huh?). Spot was mostly white, with a large brown spot across his back. Spot loved to hunt squirrels, and we took him (or he took us) into the woods several times to find some. Several times, Spot would run to a tree and jump up on it, barking and howling to indicate a squirrel. If Slim didn't see a squirrel, he would beat Spot for a false alarm. I didn't know anything about training squirrel dogs, but that didn't look right to me.

"Slim, why are you hitting Spot like that?"

"Because he has to learn not to bark like that if there's no squirrel in the tree."

"Well, maybe there was one, and we just didn't see it."

"No, if there had been a squirrel there, I would have seen it."

There was no arguing with Slim, and besides, what did I know? So, I let it ride. I felt sorry for Spot though, and made it a point to give him a few hugs and pets. At one point, Slim got mad at me for that, and hit me with a light backhand.

"Stop that. He's got to learn to mind, and not bark when there's no squirrel."

I had had enough of his rough treatment, and lashed back with a fist to his jaw, and a shove that knocked him over. I knew I was in for it then. His look told me it was time to beat a hasty retreat, so I took off running. Fortunately, I could run faster than he, and he finally wore himself out. The chase also reduced his anger, and we were okay after that. Also I noticed that he never hit me again.

Slim's dad smoked Chesterfield cigarettes and would usually leave an open pack on a shelf above the stove in the kitchen. Several times, Slim would take a couple of cigarettes and we would smoke them behind the shed. We would always be careful to not take too many so his dad would not notice.

The next day Slim said, "Hey Mom, take us squirrel hunting, will ya?"

"Oh Slim, it's so hot. I don't want to go out there today. Besides, I already have something else planned for supper."

After several more entreaties, Mrs. Jenkins finally gave in, and we tramped into the woods. The ground around there is hardscrabble; mostly clay, and very rocky. The woods are mostly oak and hickory, and there is very little underbrush, so it was easy walking after we entered the woods. This was my first hunting experience, so I was really keen to observe what was happening. Also, I always enjoyed being in the woods and tried to observe all the plants and animals around. I discovered several types of moss and lichens that I had never seen before and there were lots of large rocks and boulders to look at. I'm afraid I spent a lot more time looking down at the ground than up in the trees for squirrels.

Mrs. Jenkins was a good shot and it was not long before she had shot two squirrels with her twenty-gage shotgun. We came back to the house and I watched her as she skinned and gutted the squirrels.

"Ok, let's get you two washed up before dinner."

Mrs. Jenkins got out a small five-gallon wash tub, put a little water in it from the well, and set it down on the kitchen floor. Then she told us to take off our clothes except for our underwear. Of course, Slim already knew the drill and was stripping off his clothes as she spoke. I was quite a bit slower, being used to taking a bath in a real tub, by myself in a private bathroom, so I was a little apprehensive about this arrangement.

Since Slim was already down to his skivvies, and had stepped into the tub, I could hardly refuse. When Slim was clean, I stepped into the tub. Mrs. Jenkins rubbed a washcloth with soap and started scrubbing my face and neck.

"We'll start at the top and wash down as far as possible, then start at the bottom and wash up as far as possible. When I'm done with that I'll turn around. You take off your skivvies, and wash 'possible'." Ok, now I felt better. I had wondered how that was going to turn out. As I was washing 'possible', she said, "Be sure and check yourself for ticks." It was a good thing she had said that, because I had a couple of them climbing through the nether region.

That evening, we had squirrel for supper. I did not care for the gamey taste, and really did not like having to spit out the shot.

"Don't like squirrel, huh?" said Mr. Jenkins.

"I'm just really not hungry."

Everyone laughed, because they knew I was lying.

Mrs. Jenkins cooked on a wood stove, and I think they heated the house with a wood stove as well. Slim and I went out to the wood lot next door and with a couple of axes cut down a few small oak trees to be used as firewood. We also stripped some loose bark from a few shagbark hickories to use as kindling for the stoves. We filled up several paper grocery bags with the bark and cut the trees into firewood length and stacked the wood next to the shed for use later that fall. That evening I felt a little more at ease with the 'possible' washing, and tick checking.

Slim did teach me a marketable skill; how to make farts at will. I had been able to make the sound for some time, and Vernon and I had great fun with it as a way to get on the nerves of our parents, and astound and amaze our friends. That just involved cupping a hand under an armpit and flapping an elbow up and down quickly. That worked especially well if one were hot and sweaty, and had the added benefit of expelling our body odor from under our arms along with the sound, yielding a multi-sensational experience of both sound and smell.

Slim, though, could squeeze one off from the business end, seemingly at will. We would be walking along, and he would pause, lift a leg and pull a grimace and say, "here comes one", and sure enough, a loud rumble would emanate from his trousers, along with a cloud of toxic gas.

"I can do that any time I want."

"No, you can't. Everybody farts once in a while. People just usually try to hide it."

He smacked me on the shoulder. "Yes, I can. I can fart whenever I want to."

"Okay, smart aleck, do it again – right now."

Slim stopped, went through the same procedure, pause, lift, grimace, and sure enough – another explosion.

"Wow. How do you do that?"

"You saw me. You have to concentrate, and squeeze your stomach."

I tried that, went through the procedure; pause, lift, grimace – nothing. However, not used to failure, and with a strong motivation, I practiced all afternoon. After several abortive attempts, I finally succeeded. A rather puny effort, but with further practice, I was able to render a rather respectable (at least in the company I was keeping) result. Not only that, I got to the point that I could produce several toots in rather short order. Pretty soon, Slim and I were walking happily down the road producing a veritable symphony of sounds and smells that would have made our mothers proud. (!)

I am not at all sure that I had any positive influence on Slim but he turned out alright. On the other hand, their family taught me some things about how other people live that I had not considered before. They 'made do' with a lot less, and had to be rather clever at using what they had. They did not waste things that many of us just throw away. Also,

Slim turned out to be a very good friend who taught me some things about sharing and being a friend.

Gathering Eggs

You might think, with all the chickens we had around, that there would be eggs to gather, and you would be right. Baskets and baskets of eggs were gathered every day, and brought to the basement to be washed, candled[3], graded and sold; or washed, sanitized and assembled into the trays for the incubator, depending on whether they were to be used directly as food, or hatched into more chickens.

As I watched my brother and father gather all those eggs, I wanted to help also. Since I could not carry one of those heavy baskets at that time, I decided I could carry a few eggs in my pockets, then one in each hand, to the basement. Not much of a plot here, is there? After I stuffed an egg in each front pocket, and had one in each hand, I began walking very carefully to the basement, a distance of about 75 yards. Before I got any distance at all, I had egg yolks and whites running down both legs, and my jeans were soaked. Big help I was!

Our laying hens were free range chickens. Although we had a rather large chicken house for them with roosts and nesting boxes, the chickens were also free to roam around outside in a fenced-in area as well. At night, they came into the house, and we closed the door.

As I grew older, I was able to carry one, then two, of the baskets, and continued to help with gathering the eggs, which were usually found in the nesting boxes. However, there were always some on the floor and some outside that we had to find, so we always made the walk through the building, then around the outside.

There would usually be up to four or five eggs in each nesting box

---

[3] Candling is the process of shining a light through the eggshell, to determine if the egg contained a bloodspot or other abnormality. The presence of a bloodspot would indicate the egg was fertile. Although that did not make the egg inedible, it certainly would make it unappetizing to the customer, so it would be discarded.

compartment, as several hens would share them. If a hen were still sitting in the box, I just reached under her to gather however many eggs were under her at the time. Of course, the hens became quite used to me visiting every day, and a few of them developed some very friendly habits. One hen would always wait for me, and as soon as I would thrust my hand under her, she would stand up and lay her egg into my hand. Then she would cluck contentedly and hop out of the box. There were a couple other hens that would fly up onto my shoulders unbidden, and ride around the hen house with me while I did my job.

If you have ever dreamed of the idyllic vision of living on a quaint farm and listening to the hens cluck and a rooster crow at the crack of dawn, then you have no idea of the noise we lived with. Hundreds of roosters crowing, not only at dawn, but all during the day, along with thousands of hens cackling and squawking, causes quite a racket. What begins around dawn with a single cockle-doodle-doo quickly turns into a cacophony that could wake the dead. Add to that a few hundred turkeys gobbling noisily at every minor disturbance in the air, and the mooing of a couple of cows that need to be milked – I'm surprised our neighbors didn't run us out on a rail.

Pets

While Jerry had all kinds of wild and wooly animals as "pets", we also had more mundane creatures that almost anyone would recognize as pets. Lady was the first pet I can remember. I think I must have been around three or four. She was a Black Labrador mix, with a white streak under her chin and down her chest. She was a good dog to stay in the fenced-in back yard, so she was left unchained.

We had a sandbox in the backyard, about four feet square, and she would often make her bed there in the cool sand. She was, like most Labs, very loving and gentle with us and loved to play whatever games we were playing. If we were digging in the sandbox, she would join in.

If we were trying to play ball, she would think of it as a game of 'fetch', and then 'keepaway'.

One morning, Mom told me that Lady had a special surprise for me in the backyard. I ran out the back of the house, through the back porch and down the steps to the yard, and there was Lady in the sandbox, curled around a bushel of little puppies! There were black ones and spotted ones, and one that looked just like her, complete with the white stripe down the neck and chest.

The puppies were still wet, and I can still smell the earthy aroma of the new birth as I write this. Lady looked up at me with a very satisfied look on her face. I had been warned that she might be protective of her babies, and that I should not get too close, but she obviously trusted me as a member of her pack, and welcomed me to pet her and each new member of her family.

I was thrilled, of course, and picked up each little new life in turn to caress and hug to me. The one I fell completely in love with though, was the one that looked like his mother. I named him immediately, and thought that the only appropriate name would be Laddie. He and I became inseparable, and we played most of every day together.

Laddie had more of a roaming streak than his mother though, and would occasionally climb over the fence. Notice I said 'climb'. The fence was too tall for him to jump over, and we were puzzled for a long time about how he could get out, until I actually saw him climbing over one day. He would stand up on his hind legs and put his front paws on the wire of the fence, then just walk up the wire mesh with both front and rear paws until he reached the top. Then he would struggle over the top, teeter there for a second, and hop down on the other side.

All too soon I turned six, and it was time to go to school. No more spending hours and days playing with my favorite friend. Laddie would bark and cry when I told him good-by in the mornings, and more than a few times he followed me to school. Mr. Allen, the new principal, and Mrs. Evans, my teacher, both knew Laddie and that he was my pet, so they told me to round him up and get back to school as soon as possible, which I did. When I took him back to the yard he was ecstatic, until he realized that I was going to have to chain him up and leave, when he would start crying again. It was heart-breaking for a little kid.

After a few times of this, I was informed that I needed to come up with a more permanent solution; they couldn't keep letting me out of school to take care of my pet. So, Laddie had to be chained up before I left for school every day. Pretty soon that turned into being chained all the time, because he would escape almost as soon as I would let him loose.

One day Laddie once again climbed the fence to follow me to school. He made it over the fence, but his chain was not long enough for him to reach the ground on the other side, so he hanged himself. Dad found him later, and buried him before I returned from school, so I wouldn't see him hanging there.

I was crushed by the loss. We would have more dogs, cats, and other animals as I grew older, but I was never as close to any of them as I had been to Laddie. We had been soul mates. To this day, tears come to my eyes as I am thinking of him.

Another aspect of that experience that I did not give enough thought and appreciation to, is the fact that my dad was compassionate enough to try to shield me from the worst aspects of the loss. He never said anything about it, either at the time or after. He just quietly did what he thought he should do to help me, and left it at that. I wish I had expressed my appreciation to him while he was alive.

Friends and Neighbors

There was a family that lived upstairs on the left side of the house, named Peterson. It was great to have them, because Janice and Vernon were my best friends. Janice was about my age, and Vernon was a few years younger. When we wanted to play outside, which was every day in the summertime and most days in the winter, we didn't have to call anyone, or go to another house to see if someone was home. We were all there, and all we had to do was just go outside. If the others weren't outside, they soon would be when they heard the first kid go out the door. We were together every day, and mostly got along well. If we began fighting, Norma Jean, their mother, would call them into the house. That would be the end of the playing for a while. Although she never said a cross word to me, I usually felt bad because I knew the fight had been as much or more my fault as theirs, and they were the ones being punished. Of course, there would be much crying and protesting about the unfairness of it all, but we learned a very valuable lesson. When we had a disagreement, we tried to settle it quietly, without creating such a stir that the "adults" became aware. Without our knowing it, peaceful conflict resolution became part of our skill set.

The adult Petersons, Norma Jean and John (Pete), were also friends with my parents. Because we all got along so well, we sometimes went on picnics together. One warm summer day when I was about 5, we traveled to Meramec State Park near Sullivan for a picnic. We had to travel in two cars, since there were five of them and seven of us at the time. Between Norma Jean and Mom, we were amply supplied with fried chicken, baked beans, potato salad and a couple of pies. Blankets were spread out on the ground and we had a great feast close to the playground near the lodge. Then we had a wonderful time on the swings, see-saws, merry-go-round and just playing tag, before the adults decided it was time to go home.

Puppies! Lady's new litter. Laddie is against my leg.

Three amigos – Vernon and Janice Peterson, with me. I am wearing a jumpsuit sewed by Mom, out of flour sacks

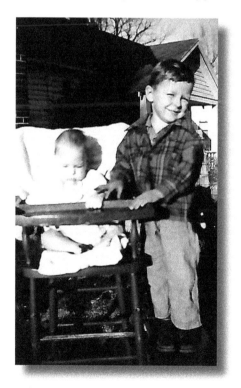

Jane's debut in front yard at hatchery, with me

The moms and dads packed up the blankets and baskets of leftover food (there wasn't much of that) and put them in the trunks, then parceled out the kids to the two cars. I watched them leave the parking lot from where I was still swinging away, not worried in the least that I had been left behind. The Petersons naturally assumed that the Landwehrs had me, and Mom assumed that I was riding home with Janice and the other Petersons. After they had turned onto Highway 66, and several miles down the road, Mom evidently looked back to the Peterson vehicle and didn't see me in it. She told Dad to pull over, and Mr. Peterson pulled in behind Dad. She got out and rushed back to the other car, affirming her worst nightmare: they had left me behind.

She was hysterical. She rushed back to our car. "We've left him back at the park! Someone could have taken him by now. Turn around, Floyd, we have to get back there right now." So they flew back to the park as fast as their wheels could carry them, and drove up to the lodge. I saw them drive up; I was still swinging and somewhat sorry to see them come back. Mom rushed over, picked me up and carried me back to the car.

I didn't like the ramp in front of the house because it made the house look like a business (which it was) instead of a nice home. The ramp also precluded the presence of a nice front yard, which everyone else in town had. However, the ramp made a great place to play several games, like Simon Says, and Mother May I, as well as a great race track for model cars. We could usually be found on that ramp in the mornings and evenings, when the sun wasn't beating on the south-facing concrete.

Many mornings during good weather an old man would come by, walking toward downtown. He was not much more than five feet tall, very overweight, and rocked side to side as he caned his way along the sidewalk. He always wore the same thing; blue work pants, a blue work shirt, old leather work shoes and suspenders. In cooler weather, he would add a denim jacket.

One of us would usually say hi to him, and he would wave his cane to us. Occasionally we would tease him by pretending to block his path. He would counter by pretending to lunge at us with his cane. We would act scared and scatter and he would continue walking, all of us laughing at the great fun.

Hours later, in the late afternoon, he would come back the other way. Not being the sharpest knives in the drawer, and never having seen a drunk before, it took us awhile to realize that it was not a good idea to do the same teasing routine as in the morning. We noticed that he was not motoring with a very steady gait and would sometimes pause, or take a step backward. When we tried to do the same skit as before, we finally noticed that he would not always see us, and when he did see us, he might become angry. Worse, we almost made him fall once. After that, we confined our teasing routine to the morning walks.

Florence lived next door on the east side of us, and lived with her mother. Florence was a telephone operator and walked to the Bell Telephone Company building downtown where she worked. She and her mother were very nice, quiet ladies, who always greeted me with a smile and a pleasant 'hello'. Like most people at that time they had a substantial garden behind their house, and I sometimes helped them pull weeds or hoe. One day our first-grade class all marched down to the "telephone office" to learn about telephone operators, and it was a very pleasant surprise to see Florence sitting on her high stool with her headset on, and all those wires and plugs arrayed in front of her. After that, when I would pick up the telephone and hear the voice say "number please", I always imagined it was Florence, even though it could have been any of the six or so operators that worked there.

As a side note, I don't remember ever initiating a telephone call until I was a teenager – fourteen or fifteen. It's possible that I did, but it is not in my memory. If I wanted to talk with someone, I merely went to their house. If they weren't home, I walked back. I mention this because I doubt if any young person today could imagine doing without instant electronic communication. When I see a small group of people today, and every one of them is speaking to someone else on their mobile phones, it strikes me as rude to be with a group of other people and yet be ignoring them all and paying attention to someone else altogether, who is not even there.

We had one telephone in the house and our phone number was 128. It was one of those old, black, clunky affairs. The telephone was located on a little shelf in our dining room and was used by our family of course but also for the hatchery business, so there was an extension in the office of the feed store. Because of the business use, personal calls during the day were not encouraged. In addition to that, nobody else in the house (none of the renters) had a telephone, so our telephone number was given out to other people as the contact number for them as well. If a call came in for one of the Petersons, we would have to put the phone down and run upstairs, knock on the door and tell them they had a call. They would then follow us back downstairs, take the call, thank us and leave. Of course, once in a while, one of them would need to make a call, and would knock on the door and ask permission to use the phone. Sherman was one of the renters upstairs, and he had an oil company distributorship. Periodically he would be expecting a delivery, and they would always call ahead in the evening before they got there, so that Sherman could go to his oil storage facility and unlock everything for them. Sherman would let us know that he was expecting that call, and that was also a subtle hint that we were not to tie up the phone with personal calls. Just like with the other calls, we would go get him when the call came in and he would follow us back down the stairs to take the call.

My friends in the house next door were an older, retired couple. We met them just a few pages back. Although I didn't know it at the time, Roy was suffering from congestive heart failure. Looking back now, I am in awe of his stamina and work ethic, even in the face of that debilitating disease. He would work in his enormous garden every day, no matter how hot. One day though, when I went to his house to help him and his wife in the garden, as I often did, he was not outside. It was deadly hot that day, and as I helped Lula pull weeds, I heard Roy's voice from the back of their house calling my name. He was standing at their back door, obviously in distress, and clutching his chest. He yelled at me to get his wife's attention, which I did. She moved as fast as she could to the house, and as I entered the back door with her, Roy was back in bed in great pain. Lula gave him a very small pill (nitroglycerin) with a drink of water, and he laid back, breathing heavily, and groaning pitifully. I asked if he was going to be okay, and he nodded weakly. Lula suggested that maybe I should go on outside and play. I was deeply concerned for Roy, but did as I was told.

Roy survived that attack, but it was not long before another one hit him from which he did not recover. That was a deep loss for me, as I truly did consider him my best friend. The age difference between us did not seem to matter to either of us. We often had spent many hours together, and it seemed as natural to me as any of my other personal relationships. He had never treated me like a child, but had always carried on conversations with me as an equal. Not everyone did that, especially back then. Many adults, including my own grandparents, had the attitude that children should be "seen but not heard", and had little to say to us.

One of Roy's stories was about a trip that he had taken on a motorcycle when he was young. First, I was astounded to hear that Roy had owned a motorcycle. He was, after all OLD, and old people didn't do such things in my mind. Second, I was surprised to hear how difficult it was to navigate in the 1920s. In 1920, there were about three million miles of road in the United States. However, only about 36,000 miles of that were 'auto-friendly', and most of them were not named or numbered, except for those in and around cities.

That was hard for me to fathom, since we had Main Street, Pickle Ford, Peacock Road, and Route 66. But even worse, there were no maps to speak of. He told of needing to make sure he always had plenty of gas, because he would quite often follow a road only to find it a dead-end, or curve in the opposite direction in which he was headed. Many times he had to stop at a farm house to ask directions and plead to buy a gallon of gasoline. Many roads back then had names invented and known to the locals, but unpublished anywhere.

Behind Roy's house, and sitting next to our driveway, was a very small outbuilding that could have been a servant's quarters at one time. It was just a single room, perhaps 8 feet by 12 feet in size. There was no insulation, inner wall or ceiling, and it was heated with a small wood stove. There was a sink, but no toilet facilities. Roy rented this building to an old man that I only got to know briefly, and have always wished that I had been more active in getting to know him better, because I am sure he had many stories to tell. His legs were very bowed, and he walked with considerable difficulty, using a cane; sometimes two canes.

His hands were gnarled and twisted, to the point that it was difficult for him to even hold his cane.

He told me that he had spent most of his adult life in Wyoming and Colorado, as a cowboy. He said that he had broken every finger in both hands, at different times, and that he also had broken an arm and both legs in various falls and mishaps while tending cattle and mending fences. Of course, he could have told me anything, but his condition seemed to be consistent with what he told me. I watched him splitting wood one day for his wood stove, and it was almost painful just to watch. He could barely bend over to pick up a buck and set it on the splitting stump without falling over. Then he could only take a partial swing of the double-bladed axe because of his unsteadiness. I was impressed though, that he was pretty accurate with the axe blows, and usually completed a split with one swing. I carried an armful of wood into the small hut for him, and he thanked me with great kindness. After that, I decided to help him also, so I made it a point to keep a stack of split wood by his door every day. One day, I noticed he was just gone. I suspect he died in the cabin and had been taken away, but I will never know for sure.

On the other side of our house lived Florence Chapman and her mother, whom we met a few pages ago. Two houses down from them lived another retired couple, named Monte. They were both musicians; he played the baritone, and she played piano. In fact, she was the church pianist at the First Baptist Church, where we attended. More importantly on a daily basis, she was the neighborhood snitch. She considered it her God-given job to watch for any misdirected behavior on the part of any neighborhood ruffians, and to bring that to the attention of the parents of the offending brats. We would often feel the righteous stare when we were playing in the back yard, and all too often we would be summoned to the house for punishment, based on the righteous indignation of Mrs. Monte.

On the other side of the Monte house, and directly across the street from the church, was the IGA grocery store. A very nice family owned the store, and since it was only four lots from our house, I was sent to it several times a week to buy a loaf of bread, sack of flour, or sugar or some such. I was sorry to see it move sometime later, when they expanded and moved out to Highway 30 into a new supermarket.

Next to that sat a rather small, low concrete block building, about the size of a one-car garage. Across the front of the building was a sign advertising a job printing company. The owner was a somewhat round, friendly man, with an easy smile and a pleasant voice. He ran a very small job printing business in the building, which I am sure was not very prosperous, because he very seldom had a lot to do. That probably accounted for his willingness to talk with Vernon and me no matter when we happened to drop in. I loved to go there, because the old building was full of interesting things. There were ancient printing presses, manually operated and fed one sheet of paper at a time, giant knives that cut stacks of paper to the right size, an old roll-top desk where the owner did his paperwork, and racks of movable, hand-set type in different fonts, all facing backward and upside down.

The Hatchery

Our basement housed the hatchery part of Dad's operation. The incubators were essentially room-sized wood boxes, and there were several of them. Each incubator had three compartments. The first two held eggs during the first two weeks of incubation. The third compartment was for the last week of incubation, and was kept at a slightly different temperature and humidity than the other two. Each of the compartments was filled with racks that held trays in which the eggs had been loaded. These racks were turned automatically every so often to keep the eggs at an even temperature, and to keep the egg whites from sticking to the shell.

Saturday was a busy day. In the morning, we made the shipping boxes we would need for the new chicks hatching that day. In the afternoon, Dad loaded his truck and ran his feed route. He delivered feed to several farmers and picked up the eggs they had collected during the week to be set in the incubators for hatching. Upon returning from the feed route the eggs had to be carried to the basement and stacked near the egg tray loading table. After supper it was time for the "hatch to come off". The finish section of the incubator was turned off and the doors were opened. Chicks were unloaded into the boxes we had made that morning. At this stage, the boxes were just filled up – no effort to count was made. The boxes were staged for the next step in the process to be done on Sunday morning. We'll talk more about the hatch in a couple of minutes.

It was the kids' job to make the shipping boxes, and it was one of my favorite chores. I got up and dressed quickly, and went to the kitchen to have my breakfast of Wheaties and cream – yes, cream. Every morning and evening, my oldest brother, Jerry, would milk the Jersey and Guernsey cows (one of each), and put the milk in the refrigerator. By morning, the cream would have risen to the top of the milk from the evening before, and I would skim that off to put on my Wheaties. Cholesterol? Never heard of it!

Down to the basement to make boxes. There were basically three sizes of shipping box. The smallest was about eight inches by ten inches, and about six inches high. That one would hold 25 newly-hatched chicks. The other two sizes were multiples of that, and would hold 50 or 100 chicks.

Each box and lid had several round perforations that could be punched out for ventilation. In early spring when the weather was still cool, we only punched out a few holes. As the weather warmed, we gradually increased the number of holes we punched out. What was the right number? I don't remember any specific instructions, other than occasionally, Dad would look at what we were doing, and say, 'a few more', or 'a few less'. He was a man of few words.

I don't know why, but every time I went to the stack of flattened cardboard that would soon be several boxes, I would make note of the manufacturer's label printed in the center of the box: "Made by Anderson Box Company, Anderson, Indiana". So who cares? I don't know either; I just always did it. Little did I know then that I would spend most of my working life in Anderson, Indiana.

I would pick up a couple of boxes, sit down on the stack, and begin punching out the holes with my index finger. This was always fun for awhile, but after several boxes, my finger would get raw from the rough cardboard edges. Dad noticed that, and fashioned a punch out of wood that looked sort of like a tiny hammer. What would be the head of the hammer was shaped by hand to be the handle of the punch. The 'handle' of the hammer was made out of two short pieces of wooden dowel, one glued inside the other. The smaller diameter dowel at the bottom was just under the hole size to be punched out, and the larger diameter dowel was considerably larger, so that it bottomed out on the cardboard. It just sort of showed up one day; no fanfare, or 'here, use this'. Few words. Anyway, after that, I could punch holes all day.

The next step in making the boxes was to fold the sides up and staple the corners together, using a floor-mounted stapler. For the larger boxes, partitions also had to be stapled into the boxes, dividing the boxes into 25-chick compartments. I was only allowed to perform this job when, ah, …actually, I just started doing it, and nobody seemed to object too much. Training? That was mostly observation, including the first time I jammed the stapler and had to ask Dad to unjam it. I don't know how, but I never managed to staple any of my fingers to a box – not one.

The next step was to put excelsior (straw) into the bottom of each box. This came in sheets about one-half inch thick, cut just the right size to fit into the compartments. Each sheet was wrapped in brown paper. You just had to slip the paper off, and put the straw in the box. After that, the boxes were stacked up, ready to receive the chicks that were already hatching in the incubators. At the height of Dad's business, it took more than two hundred boxes to handle the hatch every week.

All that was done before noon and my part of the weekly hatch was over, so I could go out and play. While I was doing that though, some farmers who weren't on Dad's feed route were bringing in their eggs for the next hatch. We did not have our own breeding flock at that time; we sold breeding flocks to farmers from prior hatches, and they bought their eggs to be hatched in a future cycle.

All day Friday and Saturday, farmers brought in their eggs in 30-dozen cases we supplied. The eggs were taken to the basement and stored until Saturday evening.

"Dad, can I go with you today?"

"I don't know, do you have the boxes made yet?"

"No, but I could do that this afternoon."

"OK, let's go."

I loved to ride with Dad. Even though he worked at home, with the feed store and hatchery being attached to our house, it seemed he was always hard at work, or running one of his feed routes. Besides, if I rode in the truck, Dad sometimes let me shift – with his hand on top of mine on the gearshift, of course. Dad's truck was a black 1948 Chevrolet panel truck, with a neat logo on the side of it. There was a crank in the middle of the dash that opened the windshield a little bit, so you could feel fresh air on your face. The windshield was hinged at the top and latched at the bottom.

This particular route took us southeast from St. Clair on Highway 30, to Lonedell. We stopped at a couple of farms along the way and then headed south on County Highway FF. Just south of Lonedell, the road rose and curved around a ridge where we stopped at the Luebbering Store. This was one of my favorite stops. Like many places in Missouri, Luebbering was hardly even a wide place in the road. Years before, the United States Postal Service had decided it needed a post office in that general area and it chose this spot because it had a general store already.

The store had one gasoline pump that was operated by hand. It had a large glass container at the top that had a brass strip inside it on which were stamped numbers indicating how many gallons were in the container. One merely pulled a lever back and forth, which pumped gasoline up into the glass container. When the desired amount had been pumped into the container, the nozzle was then lifted off the pump and put into the fuel filler of the truck. Squeezing the handle opened a valve that then emptied the container into the truck by gravity.

I loved going into the store and smelling all the odors from the various dry goods, but what I really enjoyed was that Dad almost always bought me a pop. The Coke machine was on the porch in front of the store. It was one of those horizontal ones where you opened the lid, put your dime in the slot and then slid your soda to the dispensing corner where there was a gate-like lever. You just lifted the soda out past the lever, which dropped the dime and reset the lever. I had to let Dad get the sodas, because I could not pull hard enough to lift the soda through the gate. I usually got the soda part way up and had to stop and get a better grip. At that point the dime dropped, the lever reset, and the soda was trapped in the machine.

Inside, you could buy shoes, boots, coats, jeans, canned goods, flour, sugar, and all sorts of things. There was a big pot-bellied stove in the middle of the store and in the back was the post office. The store owner was also the postmaster, which I always thought was neat. We dropped off a few bags of feed, which the store resold for us, and went on our way.

The next stop was my favorite one. It was at Mrs. Metzger's farm, to pick up some eggs and drop off some feed. She lived in a really small one-story farmhouse. Dad would put the feed in the chicken house, and carry the cases of eggs to the truck, then she would always invite us in for cookies and milk. Dad always took the time to talk with her for a few minutes before we left; longer than at most other farms we visited.

As we left the farm, I asked Dad, "Why isn't Mr. Metzger ever at home?" I had asked this same question many times before, and Dad had always put me off or changed the subject. This time he said, "Mrs. Metzger is a widow."

"You mean, Mr. Metzger is dead? How did that happen?"

"He was spraying DDT on a windy day one time, and got very sick. A few days later, he died. That's why I talk with her whenever I see her. She is a very lonely person."

"Gee, she didn't seem lonely to me, she just seems very nice."

"She doesn't want any pity, but it doesn't hurt to be a friend, does it?"

"No, I guess not."

After leaving Mrs. Metzger's farm, with the soda, cookies and milk and the warm air, I couldn't stay awake. I laid down on the seat, with my head on Dad's right leg, and had a wonderful, secure nap. I could still smell the farms we had just left, mixed with Dad's familiar, summery sweaty odor, and everything felt right with the world. By the time we arrived back home, I was ready to finish making the boxes for the hatch.

The Hatch

At various times during the few weeks involved for chicks to hatch, Dad would have to open the doors for one reason or another to check on the progress of the hatch. Occasionally, toward the end of the incubation period, we would see an egg or two that had cracked or broken open, and the chick was obviously dead. These would be removed and disposed of, so the contamination would not affect the other eggs. Once, while watching Dad do his thing, I noticed an egg that had cracked, and there was a little hole in the egg, where the chick inside was trying to peck its way out of the egg. I decided it would be a good thing to help the little guy get out, so I began peeling away the shell for the chick. Dad stopped me right away.

"What are you doing?"

"This chick is trying to get out, and I am trying to help it along. It looks like he is having a tough time."

"Don't do that. The chick needs the work involved in getting out of the shell to build up its strength. If you help it along now, it will come out weak and will probably die."

"But, what if it doesn't have the strength to get out?"

"Then, it would die anyway, and you helping it would not change that."

I wasn't sure I believed him, but he was my dad, and he seemed to know everything about hatching and raising chickens, so it must have been true.

I was too young to attach much meaning to that episode then, but it made a significant impression on me, and later on I decided that was a good metaphor for life among humans as well. We need to experience and work through our struggles. If someone else takes ownership of those and solves all our problems for us, we don't grow.

Saturday evening was time for "the hatch to come off". The heat was turned off in the hatching chamber, the doors were opened, and the chicks were transferred to the boxes we had made. At this point, we did not bother to count the chicks, we just filled the boxes. Once all the live chicks had been transferred to boxes, it was time to clean the trays. Of course, if everything were perfect, there would be just dry pieces of shells, right? Right, well, in life not everything is perfect. So, there were infertile eggs that had just rotted for three weeks, chicks that had emerged from the shell with the last bit of energy in their tiny bodies, and just died, and some chicks that didn't have sufficient strength to punch their way through the shell and died inside. All in all, a very messy and stinky affair.

All this debris was dumped into barrels and moved outside as quickly as possible – remember, we lived right upstairs. Of course, in dumping all that stuff, some of those rotten eggs invariably burst open and blessed us with their revolting, sulfurous odor. The trays were then scraped with a wire brush, washed in a fungicide (a very strong solution of something called Par-O-San), and stacked so they would be ready for the next load. (When I was a little older, I used the Par-O-San a couple of times, full strength, on some Athlete's Foot, and it dried it up almost overnight.) The hatching chamber was cleaned out, and made ready for the two-week old eggs to be transferred into it. That transfer was made and now we were ready to load the eggs just brought in from the country.

Dad stayed up late into the night on Saturday reloading the trays with the new eggs. There was a racking table that could be adjusted in height and also could be adjusted to hold the trays at an angle, like an easel, to make it easier to reach to the far end of the tray. A label was inserted into the front handle of every tray, to identify the source of the eggs (which farmer), the date, breed, etc. Sometimes these eggs were incubated for a specific person, but usually they were eggs that dad had bought for his own trade.

Sexing

Some people wanted a mixture of hens and roosters, for various reasons. For those people, we just counted out the number of chicks they wanted and put them into a box. The law of averages would guarantee that they would get some random mixture of each. Other people however, would want only hens. These would be for flocks that were to produce eggs for human consumption, such as the eggs one would purchase in a grocery store. If that flock were to include even a small number of roosters, or cockerels, the eggs laid by the hens would be fertile. That would result in several of the eggs having blood spots on the yolks – a very unappetizing surprise. For that reason, we went through a process of separating the pullets (female chicks) from the cocks, or cockerels (male chicks).

On Sunday morning, a Chinese man would come to the hatchery and separate the pullets from the cockerels. This process was called sexing, and I was fascinated with the process. Many times, I would get ready for church early and go down to the basement to watch and to see if I could figure out what was really going on.

He would set a full box of chicks on the center of a table, with an empty box on either side. Then he would perch an empty coffee can at the center of the full box and pick up two fistfuls of chicks – perhaps three or four in each hand. The first thing he would do is point the butt of a chick in each hand toward the coffee can and squeeze each one, causing each chick to squeeze out a little missile of poop that would almost invariably land in the can (or almost). Then he would turn each chick's butt toward him, part the down, and peer intently into the chick's butt. I never could figure out what he was looking for in there. At any rate, whatever he had found in there would cause him to throw a chick into one box or the other. Amazingly, he was very accurate. We never had a complaint about mistakes in this procedure. When I think back on this now I am really amazed at the numbers. At the height of Dad's business, he was producing about 40,000 chicks every week, and most of those had to be separated by sex. That guy was looking at about 30,000 chick butts every Sunday morning!! And, he did that after doing a like number at Uncle Elmer's on Saturday evening.

After the chicks were separated and counted out in boxes to match our orders, the boxes were secured with copper binding wire. Many of the chicks were picked up on Monday by those who had ordered them, because the purchasers lived locally. However, we did receive orders from people all over the country.

When we had show-and-tell at school, I chose to describe that procedure, and started by saying I was going to tell about 'sexing'. That caused Mrs. Evans to sit right up and interrupt my monologue by asking what I was really going to talk about. She allowed me to continue, but stayed alert to cut me off if I strayed too far into dangerous territory. Remember, this was 1951, and we were only six-year olds.

There was no Federal Express or UPS then, so all our chicks were sent by Parcel Post. On Monday morning, all the boxes of chicks were loaded into our truck and taken to the Post Office. We drove around to the back, where there was a loading dock. Then we took all the boxes off the truck and stacked them inside, where they were weighed, and Dad paid the postage. Everyone knew when we had made a delivery, because the post office became very loud with all the cheeping from thousands of chicks. While we were there, I walked through the counter area to the front and checked our mail box. It was box number 98; one of the larger boxes on the bottom row, so I could reach it. I loved doing that; I felt very important, being able to operate the combination lock.

Mr. Pierce

Dad hired an old gentleman to help with the hatchery chores, such as feeding and watering the baby chickens, getting eggs ready to put into the incubators, and cleaning the cages.

Every cage had a wire mesh floor that the chicks walked on. Manure fell through the mesh onto a "dropping pan" that had to be cleaned every week. This involved dumping the contents into a wheelbarrow and then relining the pan with newspaper. The paper facilitated cleaning by keeping the droppings from sticking to the pan. Full wheelbarrows were then wheeled out to our dung heap and emptied onto the pile.

Neighbors would save their newspapers for Dad, who would go around and pick them up. They had been used to doing that because of the paper drives that had been held all through World War II. The papers were then used to line those dropping pans. I was always amused that Mr. Pierce would pick up those newspapers and actually read some of them even though they might be a year old. I asked him how much news he could get out of a paper that old. "It's news to me", he said. Then he would unfold one double page and lay it on the pan, and spit a huge gob of tobacco juice onto the paper to hold it down until he got it put back in place. I think seeing those disgusting blobs all over the place is what persuaded me not to try chewing tobacco.

Mr. Pierce was tall and slender, with a long, weather-beaten face that looked like leather. He had a full head of white hair, and an oval face with a long nose and large mouth. His ears were rather large, with a giant 'hangy down part'. Like many people back then, he did not worry overly much about finer points of grooming so he had very bushy eyebrows, and lots of hair growing out of every orifice in his head. He always wore a blue denim shirt under a pair of bib overalls. He kept his twist of tobacco in one of the chest pockets in his bibs.

Mr. Pierce was a great tease, had a wonderful sense of humor and knew lots of nonsense songs about chewing tobacco, grasshoppers, railroads, hobos, etc. He taught me several of them, and when I began to sing them around the house Mom was not happy and asked him to stop teaching me that stuff. She also told me to stop spending so much time with him. We continued to sing the songs, but were more careful to make sure Mom was not around.

It's the Economy, Stupid

Much as the market for mules declined with the end of World War I and the advent of powered agriculture, the hatchery and feed store business became quite crowded when World War II ended. There didn't seem to be enough business for the Winkler Brothers Hatchery, the MFA (Missouri Farmers Association) operation and Dad's store as well in our small town. Dad's customers were not doing well either and many did not pay their bills. Dad could not bring himself to cut off anyone's credit or to ask anybody to pay their overdue bills, so they piled up. He kept a pasteboard box (yes, the proverbial shoebox) on his desk in the hatchery in which he put the credit sale slips, and the box was full. I do not believe he ever wrote a collection letter, or dunned anybody to pay their bills to him, so the receivables became uncollectible.

In addition to that, the hatchery business was changing, with several giant corporate hatcheries taking over. Smaller hatcheries like ours were closing in droves, including the other Landwehr operations. Dad couldn't bring himself to abandon the business he had built and worked so hard on for most of his adult life, so it died a slow, agonizing death, finally resulting in bankruptcy.

Before it came to that however, both Dad and Mom tried several things to help supplement the family income. Mom went to work in the

Deb Shoe Company factory for a while, until it closed due to overseas competition. The International Shoe Company had already closed years earlier. She also worked as a cook at Lewis Café downtown, and at the White Rose and Chuckwagon restaurants in Union. She was well known for her pies, and could crank out half a dozen pies in a couple of hours while hosting a house full of friends and family. Dad went to work pumping gas at a truck stop on Route 66, called Keys Twin Bridges. Mostly he worked the night shift, so it became even more necessary for Mom and me to man the store during the day. Jerry and I performed a lot of the feed delivery that Dad had formally done. Our candy business was a part of that effort to stave off the inevitable.

When Dad had been a farmer in his younger days, hogs were known as mortgage lifters, so he decided to try raising some hogs. Since we lived in town he couldn't raise them there, so he rented some ground from 'old Mr. Stahlman' on "Happy Sock" (Happy Sac) Road. He bought 100 pigs, and we turned them loose on the farm. The lot included a large grove of oak trees so the pigs had a lot of acorns to eat, which was a good supplement to the feed we provided. Although the lot sat above the creek, there was no water on the lot so we had to manually pump water from the creek up to a large water tank in the lot. The pump had to be manually operated by pulling a lever back and forth because there was no electricity at the farm. The project was eventually abandoned because it was too difficult to maintain that herd at the remote location.

One of Dad's really good customers was Leo, a giant of a man with a gentle manner who was honest and hard-working. He always paid his bills and was very easy to work with. The problem with Leo's farm was that it was so remote. To get to his farm we had to drive a few miles west on 66, then turn onto a gravel road for a few miles until we came to his property. At that point a two-track lane departed from the county road. That lane seemed to be miles long, but my memory is probably not accurate on that.

Although we made deliveries to his home many times, one stands out for me. We had had one of those typical Missouri snowfalls that is preceded by and followed by freezing rain. Following the snow/ice storm, the weather had turned cold and windy. Jerry and I were delivering feed this time, with Jerry driving; Dad was working at the truck stop. We had traversed that two-track through a rather dense oak and hickory forest, then out onto a low meadow which was fenced in for cattle.

Jerry stopped in front of the gate and said, "open the gate, Wayne, but make sure you close it behind us, because Leo could be running cattle in this field."

"Okay." I jumped down from the truck and walked to the gate, which consisted of three strands of barbed wire. At one end the strands had been nailed to the gate post. At the other end, the wire had been fastened to a stick, with heavy wire staples. There was also a stick in the middle of the span, to hold the strands of wire apart. The free end of the "gate" was held to the other gate post by slipping the top and bottom ends of the end stick into loops of wire that had been wrapped around the other gate post.

I lifted the top loop off the stick, raised the gate assembly off the lower loop, and walked the floppy gate into the field. Jerry drove the truck through and stopped on the other side, waiting for me to secure the gate again. I did so and returned to the truck but just stood on the running board, since I knew we were going to have to repeat this procedure at least three more times. After passing through the second field, the two-track partially ascended a hill which we had to then drive around, with the truck listing about 15 degrees. At that point I had re-entered the truck, for fear of sliding off the slick running board, and because I had become quite cold. We were fully loaded and I thought we might sink into the track enough to avoid sliding down the hill, but I was wrong. Jerry had to keep steering up the hill to keep us on the track.

When we got about half-way around the hill the track descended into a dry creek bed which lay about thirty inches below the grade. Just prior to arriving at the creek, we encountered the last gate. I got out of the truck and did my thing, and Jerry slowly descended the creek bank, then gunned it to get up the far bank. As soon as he had reached relatively flat ground he stopped and waited for me to close the last gate, walk across the creek and re-enter the truck.

We were now faced with the final hurdle; a fairly steep grade of about 100 yards in length, at the top of which were the house and barn. We had maybe three truck lengths of flat ground before the grade started, so Jerry accelerated as fast as he could without spinning the wheels and attacked the hill. We made it perhaps 20 yards before the tires lost purchase and just began spinning. Because the hill also had a side component to it, the truck also started to wander off the track. He stopped, backed up to the bottom and tried again. And again. And again.

Finally, it became apparent even to me that we weren't going to get up that hill. We walked up the hill to Leo's house and told him of our situation.

"Hi, Jerry, did you bring me some feed?"

"Hi, Leo, yeah, we brought a truck full, but we can't make it up that last hill. There's not enough room to turn around, and I don't think I can back through that creek, so I don't know what we're going to do. Can you give us some help?"

"Sure, sure, I'll break out the tractor and maybe I can help by pulling you up the hill. I have a really stout log chain. Can we hook onto you?"

"Yeah, we can wrap the chain around the frame."

"Okay then, let's go. Let me put on my boots first though."

So, Jerry and I walked back down the hill, and we both got back in the truck. I was now half frozen and my feet were wet – I didn't have a pair of proper weather-proof boots or insulated socks. Leo came rumbling down the hill with his big Case tractor and hooked up a humongous log chain to the truck frame. He got back onto the seat and slowly took up the slack then brought his arm down in a 'forward-ho' movement. Both Jerry and Leo hit the gas and we started up the hill. After climbing up the hill about 50 feet the wheels started slipping on both the truck and the tractor. Jerry thought he saw Leo wave for him to stop, so he let up on the gas and started to let the truck drift back down the hill. Leo became aware of this as his tractor was being dragged back down the hill, so he relented and followed the truck back to the bottom. He got off the tractor and ambled back to the truck.

"Jerry, we need for DeWayne to get out and stand between the truck and tractor, off to the side, and let us know when the wheels are starting to spin too much, and call out when we should go and when to back up. We are not pulling together."

"Good idea, Leo. Wayne (he never did learn what my real name was), get out and stand over there off the lane, and signal us when to pull and when to stop and back up."

So, I got out of the truck and stood about ten feet off the two-track, in about a foot of soft snow (afraid to stand any closer, because both the tractor and truck would occasionally slew to one side or the other as they tried to gain traction getting up the hill). I slowly circled my hand, signaling Leo to take up slack, then lowered my arm in a 'forward-ho' movement, at which both tractor and truck tried to accelerate. They progressed only about thirty feet up the hill before they both began to spin out, so I crossed my arms telling them to stop, roll back to the bottom and try again.

On about the third or fourth cycle of this, they were spinning out again, and I once again gave the signal to stop and back up. Jerry got the signal in the truck, but Leo must have been looking elsewhere and did not, so he continued to pull, even as the truck started to back up. The chain snapped taut, and the giant hook broke away from the chain with a loud pop that sounded like a cannon. I felt a slight breeze as the hook sailed past my head, swept my hat off and continued into the woods. At first I was shocked, then I started to shake uncontrollably, as the realization of what just happened set in. That could have taken my head off!

Both Jerry and Leo got down from their vehicles and rushed over to me, to make sure I was alright. Then we tramped through the trees, brush and ankle-deep snow for several minutes, looking for that hook. We never did find it.

Leo heated his house with wood, and had a pretty significant ash heap close to his house. He suggested we try to spread that on the trail to get some additional traction, so we brought back about half a yard of that, and spread it on both tracks where the truck had been slipping, and on up the hill until it flattened out. That did the trick. After making it to the top of the hill, Leo invited us into his house to warm up before we went back out and unloaded the truck into his barn. My pant legs and socks were completely soaked from tramping around in the snow and it took some time before the tingling in my hands and feet subsided. We dried socks and gloves on the wood stove, and drank some much-appreciated coffee. Since the five-ton load was all in 50-pound bags, it took us awhile to offload the 200 bags, walk them into the barn and restack them.

The return trip was not nearly as exciting as the trip going out.

School

I couldn't wait to go to school. I was the fourth child, so I watched every day as my three older siblings went off to class, and it seemed so magical. The entire school system was located right across the street in three buildings; one building each for elementary, middle and high school. They were roughly 1920s vintage, three-story brick buildings. I would watch every day as Jerry, Maxine and Janet joined the other children on their way to what seemed to me a wonderful experience. At various times of the day large numbers of kids would burst from the doors and plunge onto the playground amid shouts and laughter. What fun!

Finally, it was my turn. Mrs. Evans was the teacher, and of course she let me know that she knew our family, because she had already taught Jerry, Maxine and Janet. She let me know that she hoped I would take after Maxine and Janet, and not Jerry (that sentiment followed me all the way through school). There were tags made up with our names typed on them, and taped to the top of each desk. Of course, we couldn't read, but pretty soon we all began to associate that strange jumble of letters with our names and the location of our own desks. Since my birthday was at the end of August, I was one of the youngest in the class, but I was ready to learn.

As we began to learn our letters and some words I was doing great with words like cat and dog. Then it came time for us to be able to write our names. Oh, my gosh!! My name has fifteen letters. Why couldn't I have been named Billy Smith, or Butch Jones? We were all called to the blackboard and told to write our names on the board. I rushed to the blackboard to secure a spot really close to my desk so I could peek at the tag on my desk. Most of the kids were able to write their names the first day without too much trouble. However, it took me almost a week to be able to write mine without cheating with a peek at my desk. Finally, I was able to do it on my own – what a great feeling.

It was hot that September in Missouri, and the school did not have air conditioning so the classrooms were stifling. Most of the boys wore jeans, but I noticed one kid had shorts on so I thought that might be a good idea. The next day I also wore shorts and came face to face with the reality of peer pressure. Several of the kids laughed at me and ridiculed me with the taunt that only LITTLE kids wore shorts. That was a bad day for me and the last day I wore shorts anywhere until I was a Junior in high school. Even then I had to be persuaded that 'everyone was wearing Bermuda shorts now, and what's wrong with me?'

The situation with the shorts was really weighing heavily on my mind and I became much more conscious of doing what it took to 'be cool'. Butch helped me out. Butch was cool. Butch wore Levi's and a white T-shirt every day so I did too (except I just had Wranglers and Lees). Butch kept a pack of cigarettes rolled up in his sleeve (except in school, which wasn't allowed). I knew that wouldn't fly at my house, so I didn't do that, but I was tempted. Butch kept kitchen matches in his pocket so I did too. These were great because, as he taught me, you could strike these on your zipper or even cooler, with a flick of your thumbnail. Butch had a switchblade, but I didn't know how to acquire one of those so I had him get me one. It had a fake pearl handle and was long enough that it almost stuck out of the top of my pocket, but now I was cool – I had matches and a switchblade. Butch knew several nasty poems, so I memorized those. I think my parents would have been horrified.

Along the way an interesting thing happened. I eventually noticed that Butch was not much of a student. Most of my friends were not really into matches and switchblades and rude poems. Over time I realized that I wanted to be a good student, because I loved learning and I never could see the benefit of carrying a switchblade or all those matches around, so we gradually parted company.

Mrs. Evans let us know that we each needed to know our own home telephone number, and we would have to tell her what it was. She told us a couple of days ahead of time so we could ask our parents, if we didn't already know it. I didn't need to ask anybody. I already knew where to find our telephone number. Everybody knew that telephone numbers were always printed on the doors of commercial trucks, so I just looked at my dad's truck and found it – BL 14,000. When I proudly announced our number as BL 14000 she questioned me about that, but I stuck to my answer. She encouraged me to confirm that with one of my parents. After doing that and when asked the next day again about my telephone number, I had to sheepishly acknowledge that it was really 128. That's it – just three digits.

Easter

Our house (and consequently the hatchery and feed store) were located right across the street from the school buildings. Most of the kids walked to school every day so they passed right by our house on the way. Since the war demand for chickens and eggs had died down Dad's business had been really struggling, and he decided he could possibly gain a little more income by selling school supplies and candy. So he built some narrow racks for supplies like paper, tablets, notebooks, pencils, pens, ink, erasers, etc, and hung that on the wall opposite the sale counter. He also built a large box divided into little cubes for candy. He set the box, which was about 2-feet by 4-feet and 3 inches high, on a table at the end of the counter. In no time the word got around and kids began stopping in before school with their pennies, nickels and dimes to buy some candy, and occasionally some school supplies.

Even at six years old I could make change, because I had been helping in the feed store for some time. So I got up a little early every school day and helped with the candy sales for about half an hour before school started. The store was always packed with kids jostling to get close to the candy counter. With that many kids and in a poor community, theft was a constant problem, so we were always on alert to spot anyone trying to make off with candy or supplies. I almost always confronted at least one person every day.

Spring was always the big hatching season because everyone wanted to start new flocks then. Farmers typically wanted only hens because they wanted the chickens to produce eggs for eating, not hatching. Even if they wanted the chickens to produce meat, hens were the most desired because the eggs came along for free. Consequently, and especially in the spring there were lots of surplus cockerels, or roosters, that couldn't be sold. Coloring eggs for Easter was always a big thing so Dad hit on the idea of coloring chickens.

We had purple, pink, red, blue, green, and seemingly every other color of chick for sale, and Dad displayed them near the candy starting about three weeks before Easter. Of course, who could ignore a purple chick peeping away and looking so cute. We sold them for a nickel and put them in tiny paper bags, just like we did for the candy. Everyone had to have one. The only trouble was, we sold them to the kids in the morning before school. When I got to school the first morning, I saw that Mrs. Evans had made everyone put their chick against the wall away from their desks, to minimize disruption. However, every chick was cheeping for all it was worth and the noise was pretty distracting.

Mrs. Evans was pretty shrewd, and decided that since learning would be somewhat problematical in this situation, she would take advantage of it and we did another show-and-tell. She asked me to start by telling the class how we got those chickens to be all those pretty colors, and then she asked the other students to tell how they were going to take care of their new pets.

Being the very observant and precocious child that I was, I told the class that it was all very simple. All one had to do was to color the eggs as normal, then when they hatch the chicks came out the same color as the egg.

"Really?!", said Mrs. Evans. "That is very interesting. Why don't you go home today and ask your parents for some more detail about how it is done, and tell us about it tomorrow?"

I really couldn't see that that was necessary, but then I thought, 'ok, I really haven't watched them color the chickens, so maybe I can pick up some more to tell. I had to do something; I had already told everything I knew today, and needed some more information for tomorrow.

So, when I got home from school, I said, "Hey Mom, are you going to color some more chickens today?"

"Of course we are. We sold everything we had today, and lots of the kids said they would be back tomorrow to buy one or two."

"Well, could I watch this time?" (Never being one to want to ask for information directly).

"Sure. You could even help. We were doing that after you went to bed before, but we can start earlier."

So, after dinner was finished and the dishes had been cleaned up, mom made up several different batches of RIT dye (the same dye used to color cloth) of different colors in several bowls, like cereal bowls. Then to my surprise, dad brought in a box of chicks and they started dunking these chicks in the dye. What a surprise!

"You don't color the eggs first?"

Apparently, my super-observant, precocious mind had missed the points that one wouldn't use fertile eggs to color for Easter, or that you hard boil them before coloring, among other things. After watching Mom dip a few of the chicks, she let me do it. I picked up a chick with the legs in one hand and its beak in the other, and dipped it upside down into the warm colored liquid. Voila'! We had a bright red chick! We colored about 200 of them that evening and I went to bed a lot more tired and just a little smarter – no, a little more educated. I don't think I ever got any smarter.

The next day the same scene was played out in the classroom with little bags of chicks against the wall, and me in front of the class explaining how chicks are really colored. Mrs. Evans was much more satisfied with the second explanation, but I don't think it made any difference to most of the students, who really didn't care how they were colored; they were just cute.

Trouble wasn't over however. After school those kids who rode the bus got on with bags of cheeping chicks, and drove all the bus drivers batty. The colored chick thing lasted for another year or two, but I think the school administration finally persuaded Dad to stop doing that because of all the disruption.

Weekly Readers and Walter

I was born at the beginning of the Baby Boomer Generation, on August 28, 1945. President Truman had just announced the surrender of Japan on August 14, following the surrender of Germany in the previous May. The entire world went into a frenzy of celebration. There were ticker tape parades down Fifth Avenue in New York, other parades and parties everywhere. Men and women were demobilized from the armed forces by the thousands, and families got back together to give thanks for deliverance from the 'Huns and Nips'. In this country, Eisenhower was celebrated as the hero who had led us to victory. My younger brother was named after him; David Dwight.

Unfortunately for the world, neither WWI nor WWII lived up to the promise of being the 'war to end all wars'. Russia had been an ally of convenience during the war. Now that the conflict was over Russia was seen as another serious threat to world peace as they swallowed up East Germany and many of the Balkan countries. The Far East continued to blaze in conflict as China tried to sort itself out between two charismatic leaders. General Chaing Kai-Shek had been president of China throughout the war and ruthlessly rooted out Communists from the Chinese Nationalist Party, or Kuomintang. A gifted and charismatic communist leader, Mao Tse-Tung, led millions of communist peasants in an uprising that resulted in civil war breaking out in 1946. Mao Tse Tung eventually won out by driving General Chaing Kai-Shek and more than a million of his followers off the mainland and onto the island of Taiwan.

Hardly did that burn down to a simmer, when the Korean Conflict broke out, lasting from 1950 to 1953. Almost in the midst of that the conflict between the two Chinas resumed with the shelling by Communist China of Quemoy and Matsu, two islands off the coast of mainland China. General Eisenhower had been elected as President in 1952, and the USA supported the Taiwanese government. That support brought us very close to nuclear war again. Then in 1954, the French lost French Indochina (Vietnam) when they were defeated at the battle of Dien Bien Phu. The US almost immediately picked up the support there also in an effort to keep the Communists from making the entire area Communist. President Eisenhower thought we could keep a lid on things by sending a few advisors to help out the existing ARVN (Army of the Republic of Viet Nam) troops – right.

The two largest countries in the world, Russia and China, seemed to take over the world and turn it entirely communist. There was a palpable tension in the air all the time. There were bomb drills, air raid drills, etc, and the Cold War was in full swing. One evening, much of our little town gathered near the new high school on Commercial Avenue and watched as some Air National Guard airplanes flew over in the darkness simulating a bombing run on the school, while some of our National Guard troops manned some gigantic searchlights in an effort to spot the planes in the air. What a show – almost as good as fireworks. But the serious implications were not lost, even on the mind of this twelve-year-old. Were the Russians coming soon?

All this hysteria led the government to conclude that we needed more infrastructure to be able to move troops around, so the Interstate System was conceived and begun under Eisenhower. He had been very impressed by the German Autobahn system he had seen in Germany during the war. As part of the first phase, Route 66 was improved to be a divided highway from Chicago to Santa Monica.

The news was brought to us by a father-figure news anchor named Walter Cronkite. At the end of his news broadcasts, he would sign off with, "…and that's the way it is…" He narrated another program called You Are There, in which historical events would be described and shown, along with some educational commentary about the events. At the end of that show he would say, "And that's the way it was, on Januray 7, 1941 (or whatever date), and You Are There."

On another channel we had the Huntley-Brinkley report, with Chet Huntley and David Brinkley. One was based in Washington and gave political news, and the other was based in New York, and concentrated on financially-related news. I can still hear them sign off at the end of the program with, "Good night, David…" "Good night, Chet". At school, we followed the news through our Weekly Readers. We read about this guy named Senator Joseph McCarthy, who chaired the House Committee on UnAmerican Activities. He was rooting out Communists for us, to keep us safe (I say that with tongue in cheek now). Then there was Senator Estes Kefauver, who was looking under every rug for corruption and Mafia types.

So, after a very brief respite of celebration and ecstatic rejoicing following World War II, the country became locked into, and much more aware of, a plethora of worldwide catastrophes breaking upon our consciousness: Russian and Chinese Communist expansionism, Korea, Vietnam, the Mafia, government corruption, etc. In spite of all that, I remember the time as one of optimism, although I was aware of a large amount of angst in the adults as a result of all those factors just mentioned. I think our parents had tried to shield us from most of that.

Polio, also known as infantile paralysis, was the scourge of young people and everybody was familiar with it, especially since FDR had been struck with it and many families knew of someone's child who had contracted the dreaded disease. Our Weekly Readers showed pictures of children in iron lungs and others with leg braces. Walter talked about it on the television. The March of Dimes was dedicated to helping those who had been stricken, and to eradication of the disease. We were all given little heavy paper folders filled with little niches to be filled with dimes and turned in to the school administration. We went around begging for dimes from family and neighbors, trying to be one of those who turned in the most dimes. In 1952, we became especially scared as polio hit epic proportions resulting in 58,000 new cases in the United States, while more than 3,000 died from the disease.[4]

On March 26, 1953, we heard that someone named Dr. Jonas Salk

---

[4] http://www.history.com/this-day-in-history/salk-announces-polio-vaccine

had finally developed a vaccine to fight the disease, and that he had taken the unprecedented step of trying out the vaccine on himself and his family. Within two years, the vaccine was ready for the general population and we, along with most of the rest of the children in the country, were vaccinated. Initially, the vaccine was administered as a liquid, placed on a sugar cube. Two years after that, in 1957, the number of new cases had dropped almost 90%, to under 6,000.

Every year, all students were sent home with a card that listed all the shots and vaccinations that would be offered at the school. Our parents had to check off which ones we were to receive and sign the cards. We would return them to the teacher and on the dreaded day, we would all be assembled in the gym for 'the gauntlet'. There were shots for diphtheria, Tetanus and whooping cough, measles, and the dreaded smallpox vaccine. Clear plastic bubbles were taped over the smallpox vaccines, but still some became infected, and some kids became really ill. And besides, the vaccines themselves really hurt!

Extended Family

There were seven children in my mother's family and eight in my father's family. With a couple of exceptions, each of my aunts and uncles also had from three to six children, so we had a rather large extended family. We got together every Sunday after church, usually after lunch. Occasionally, we would also have lunch all together if there was a birthday or some other reason to celebrate. The Landwehr clan would gather on one Sunday and the Cowan clan would gather on alternate Sundays. I believe the other in-law groups did the same thing.

My dad and his uncle Elmer were always very close. Dad and Elmer had married my mom and her sister Marie, so we had double cousins. My older sisters, Maxine and Janet, seemed to be pretty close to Elmer and Marie's daughters, Betty and Ruth, so gatherings of our two families seemed to be very special. Usually, a double-deck pinochle game would start as soon as the pleasantries were concluded, lunch was finished, and we kids had gone out to play. The game would continue all afternoon with only a break for the evening meal, and then continue long into the night. Normally, we younger ones would be sprawled out all over the floor asleep before the game broke up and would have to be carried to the car to go home.

Our streetlights were plain incandescent light bulbs, with saucer-like ceramic reflectors, strung over the center of the street about 100 yards apart. These created little pools of light on the street separated by substantial areas of darkness in between. I usually ended up stretched out on the floor of the car between the front and rear seats with my back bent over the drive shaft tunnel, while everyone else sat up with their feet on me. Even asleep I could tell when we got back into town, as the streetlights caused alternating light and darkness that woke me up. I usually continued to feign sleep though, so Dad would carry me into the house.

I enjoyed visiting all my aunts and uncles, but I especially enjoyed the special times when all the Landwehr side would gather at my Grandpa Landwehr's house. He lived south of Gerald, Missouri, on Highway H, on a farm that at one time had amounted to about 160 acres. There was plenty of room for all of us to run wild all afternoon without bothering any of the adults. At Christmas there would be home-made eggnog, laced with whiskey, and it was not really monitored to ensure the youngsters didn't get into it. In warmer weather we would sit on the front porch swing in the late evening, and listen to the whip-poor-wills call out into the darkening night.

Grandpa had acquired a parrot from somewhere, and kept it in a cage in the living room. That parrot offered no end of fascination for David and me. It would say, "Polly wants a cracker.", and we would dutifully feed it a saltine or two, which was always fun. Whenever we would arrive and all troop in the front door, the parrot would start squawking something that I could not understand and Mom would mutter that she wished that parrot were dead, and for us to stay away from it. We ignored her of course, and Grandpa would just chuckle. After many times of this happening, I finally realized that the parrot was saying, "Hello, you son of a bitch!"

Grandma had one of those old telephones that hung on the wall. To make a call, you had to pick up the ear piece and turn the crank several times to ring the operator, then ask her to connect you with whomever you wished to speak. They were on a party line with six other people, and each party had a particular set of rings. You were only supposed to pick up when your particular set of rings, say two short and one long ring, sounded. Grandpa usually didn't answer the telephone but when their tones sounded he would say, "telephone, grandma---grandma, telephone!" The parrot soon picked up on that, and began to alert grandma to the telephone by saying the same thing and sounding very much like grandpa.

A man came to call on them one day, and knocked on the door. Grandma didn't move too fast and would always say, "just a minute!". When she didn't come to the door right away, he knocked on the door again, and heard the same reply – "just a minute!" After a couple more tries at that, he walked around to the window at the side of the house after knocking, and there sat the parrot, saying, "just a minute!"

As time passed, many of my older cousins also began to have large families, and there were just too many people to gather in one house, so the Landwehr Christmas celebration was held at the Gerald VFW after that. The usual crowd amounted to 125 to 150 people. It was a pitch-in, and there were always mountains of food. Ham, turkey, baked and fried chicken, meatloaf, green beans, peas, mashed potatoes and gravy, German potato salad, carrots, corn, and – oh – did I mention desserts? German chocolate cake, pies of every sort; apple, peach, lemon chiffon, coconut crème, blackberry, rhubarb, fudge, cookies of every sort. It was hog heaven. After the initial luncheon meal, we would continue to graze the loaded tables of food all afternoon. Several tables of pinochle would break out and the games would usually last late into the evening. It was another great time to catch up with family and strengthen those bonds.

Sometime in the middle to late afternoon Grandpa would sit down at one of the central tables with his refreshment, and begin handing out his gifts to all the children. Because the family was so large, this was limited to those under sixteen. Word would go out that it was time for the presents, and the children would begin to gather and form a line. He had envelopes with everyone's name on them, so nobody was forgotten. The younger kids received $1 and the older kids were given $5. That seems pretty small today but back then, that would buy a lot of penny candy.

Elda was my dad's oldest sister, and she had married a man named Fred Stumpe. They lived on a farm not very far from Grandpa Landwehr on a farm that bordered on a section of the Bourbeouse River, at a location we called Red Oak. The land on that farm was not the best, except for some bottom land along the river. The upland portion of the land was like a lot of Missouri; clay and rocky, with thin topsoil. Consequently, the crops were planted in the bottom along the river. Hay was grown a little farther up, and several cattle were pastured there as well. Their farm was split by a county road that ran in a loop from Highway H. The house was located on the higher side of the farm along with a barn, a tool shed and a pond. The yard was enclosed on the front and sides by a wrought iron fence, set into a field stone and concrete base.

They had a collie that loved to chase sticks, and she would bark incessantly until you threw one for her to chase. However, as a young child I wasn't aware of that, and her barking really scared me, so that I was too frightened to go through the yard to the house. Aunt Elda told me several times that she was friendly and just wanted to play, but in spite of the fact that I loved dogs and what she told me, I could not get past my mortal fear of that incessant barking. Finally, on one trip to their house I darted out of the car as soon as Dad pulled to a stop and gathered up as many sticks as I could carry before entering the yard. The dog was barking as usual, so before I even opened the gate I threw a stick over the fence. As the dog ran after the stick, I opened the gate and made for the house. As she came back to me with the stick and dropped it at my feet I launched another one which she immediately chased after. That gave me the opportunity to run a few more steps toward the house. I continued that way until I reached the back door, when I threw my last stick and scurried inside. Elda had been watching this performance from her kitchen window, and was laughing hysterically as I ran inside. "I think you wore her out. Look, she's lying under the tree there, exhausted. I'm sure she won't bother you any more today."

Fred's barn included a rather large hayloft for winter feeding of his cattle. It was enormous fun to climb up there and chase each other around, although the first time I encountered a blacksnake there, I was somewhat frightened. I soon discovered though, that they were more frightened of me than I of them, and they were not aggressive.

We usually brought our fishing poles to fish in the pond and always caught several bluegill, and once in a while a bass. We always threw them back, since we were just there for the day of fun, not to bring home fish.

The pond's lower bank was about 10 feet high, and offered a great place to launch fireworks. We were always at Fred's house in late July, as that was Fred's birthday (Elda always called him Daddy), and the whole family was invited. There would be tables set up in the yard, groaning under the load of fried chicken, roast beef, ham, baked beans, green beans, German potato salad, pies, cakes – enough to feed an army.

I usually had a lot of fireworks left over from the Fourth of July, and I brought them with me in a large grocery bag. Several of my cousins and I were standing on the pond bank, throwing firecrackers from the bank. I had set down my bag of fireworks on the bank behind me so that it was easy to reach inside; the bag was about the level of my chest. One of my cousins accidentally dropped his lit punk into the bag. Of course, the whole bag went off. Little pieces of the bag went sailing through the air, and the sound of the explosion was like a cannon in my ear. I couldn't hear a thing, except the deafening ringing that began with the explosion.

That was the end of the fireworks activity for that year. I went to the house with a splitting headache, to receive the tongue lashing I knew would result. An upside here was that I couldn't hear it anyway. My ears rang terribly for about a week, and I was left with a bad case of tinnitus. One of those life-changing events that was to stay with me for the rest of my life.

There was a back porch to the house, and just outside there was a large cistern. Elda and Fred didn't have a well, and no running water in the house. There was a small wash stand on the back porch, and atop that was a small porcelain wash basin. There was a small cake of lye soap along with a small hand towel. When it was time to come in and wash up, a small amount of water (about two quarts) would be drawn from the cistern into the basin. The kids would be called in to wash up after the adults had already done so. When we came in the water would already be scummy, covered with a grimy film, and the towel would be almost dripping wet. No new water was provided; we washed up with that.

Dad could see that I was about to say something about the water, and silenced me with one of his trademark grimaces that told me to shut up. Later, he explained that Fred and Elda had to preserve water, because they just had a cistern. That cistern was filled from water that ran off the roof, through a downspout that ran into it. I said, "Oh.", even though I didn't really understand what that meant. My experience was that you just turned on a faucet, and water appeared. I was not yet aware that, especially in times of drought, which are commonplace in that part of Missouri during summer months, water can become scarce.

Ralph was Mom's youngest brother, and lived in St. Clair fairly close to us. He was a supervisor for the Missouri Highway Department. He would come over to see Mom quite often, wearing his work clothes; blue cotton work shirt under bib overalls. Like many people back then, Ralph smoked cigarettes. I was always intrigued by the way he held the cigarette in his mouth. Being frugal he didn't want to waste any of it, so he didn't put it into an ash tray like many people did. He kept it in his mouth for the entire smoke. Sometimes when the smoke drifted by his eyes, he would pull his head back a little and cock it to the side. Then he would close one eye and squint with the other one. He had an uncanny ability to talk while holding the cigarette between his lips. As his mouth opened and closed the cigarette would cling to his lower lip and bounce around. When he took a breath the cigarette would continue to hang there from his lower lip, almost vertically, and then he would suck it up and inhale some more smoke. He would smoke that fag until there was almost no paper left around the tobacco, then carefully squeeze it out of his mouth and drop the last quarter inch into an ash tray or onto the floor.

Clinkers

Our house was heated with coal – bituminous, or soft coal. The furnace was in the basement, and was an enormous round structure that looked much like a short silo to me. The furnace was fed by an automatic stoker through the bottom of the firebox with an auger that in turn was fed from a hopper that held about four or five wheelbarrows of coal.

The coal was stored in a room of the basement that was roughly eight feet by ten feet. Two walls of the room were outside walls, one at the front and the other adjacent to the driveway. There was an access door close to the top of the room on that wall, through which coal was delivered from a truck. There was a normal doorway in another wall of the room that provided access to the coal from the basement. That doorway was constructed with two parallel vertical doorstops, so that wide horizontal boards could be inserted to close off the "doorway". The bottom board was inserted at a 45-degree angle, so that the bottom six inches or so was open, and the shovel could be inserted there to pick up the coal to fill the wheelbarrow.

When coal was delivered, someone had to get into the room and move some of the coal into the far corners of the room as it filled up, to ensure we could offload a complete truckload. When I was about nine years old, that became my job. I would put half of the boards in place, so that I could still climb over them, and then climb in and move the coal around. There was no coal dust, because the coal was usually wet to decrease the danger of fire from coal dust. The problem was that after crawling around on top of the coal for several minutes, my clothes, hands and face became covered with the oily coal. That presented a challenge for my mother to clean up. As the room filled up, I would continue adding boards to the doorway, until there was just enough room to crawl over the boards, and I would scramble out as the coal continued to come pouring in through the access door.

Another aspect of heating with coal is that you have to empty the furnace of the burned coal. So after filling the stoker every day, I rolled the wheelbarrow to the furnace, opened the door and pulled out the burned debris. Burned bituminous coal doesn't produce fine ash like burned wood does; it produces clinkers. These are very sharp-edged rocks of carbon that are full of holes. They look very much like volcanic lava. Some of these were about as large as a soccer ball. These were removed with a long-handled iron grabber. After putting them in the wheelbarrow, I wheeled it outside to cool, then the clinkers were dumped on the driveway. Although they are very sharp, they are also fairly fragile, so once our truck ran over them once they were reduced in size to something akin to gravel. Until I started middle school, I very often went barefooted in the summer time. As my feet toughened over the summer, I could eventually walk on those clinkers without any pain or cuts. The first few times in the spring though, I walked very slowly when I had to traverse the driveway.

The Bicycle

Like most kids, I wanted a bicycle. I had hinted a few times, but no bicycle was forthcoming. There was a trash heap behind our house, and in it I found a rusted, old bicycle that I rescued with some effort. It was in pieces, and I had to do some rooting to find them all, but eventually I had the makings of a complete bicycle. There were some challenges to overcome. Several spokes were missing from both wheels. The pieces had been lying there long enough that the axles were nearly frozen in the rims. The fenders were also rusty and in need of some sanding and paint. There was no chain, pedals or grips on the handlebar and only one tire.

Learning to ride this new acquisition was a matter of self-instruction. The first obstacle was that the bike was a 28-inch monster that was too big for me at the time. Just mounting the thing required that I first lean it against something so I could climb astride it, then I pushed off with one hand while holding on to the handlebar with the other. After a couple of tries at this on level ground, I decided that it might be easier to get going if I started at the top of a hill. Our backyard included an area with a long, gentle slope, so I walked the bike to the top of that and leaned it against a large Chinese Elm tree.

Upon mounting this great machine, I discovered that my instincts had been correct; the bike almost started itself. After several abortive trips part way down the hill, in which I almost maintained it vertical long enough to reach the bottom, I finally got the hang of it. Then I realized I had no idea how to stop it and panicked. I lost control of the thing and ran directly into another large elm tree at the bottom of the hill, causing me to slide right off the seat. That action in turn caused a vital portion of my anatomy to come into harsh contact with the fork – a very painful and memorable experience. Since the horizontal bar was higher than my inseam, I was momentarily stranded there until I fell over. After falling over, I laid there for several minutes, still astride that awful machine, in great agony and wondering why I felt I needed to ride such a monster.

That ended the training for a couple of hours, but of course I finally mastered the art of mounting, riding, braking and dismounting. Once I became proficient enough, I found I could mount the bike either by just tilting it so I could swing my leg over, or (the real feat) stand on one pedal, push off, then swing the other leg over as the bike moved out.

I took the fenders off because they were so rusty they made the whole bike look bad. However, just one short trip following a light rain caused me to reassess that decision. I found out quickly that fenders aren't there just for looks. My whole body was covered with muddy, oily splatter from the street and the stains never came out of my T-shirt. Mom was not happy.

The fenders got a quick paint job with some leftover silver paint that I found in the basement, and were reinstalled before I got on it again. Now I had a complete bike, albeit not in the same class as the Schwinns that some of my friends had. Still, it got me around.

Somebody up there likes me

Mom and Dad bought us a swing set that was installed in the back-yard. It was the typical lawn ornament, with a couple of swings, a set of rings, and a slide. After sitting in the sun for several months, the metal bottom of the slide would become oxidized and a little dirty, causing it to become somewhat 'sticky', and not so fast. Sometimes friction would even stop you midway down the slide, and you would have to push yourself to the bottom. We used to save up our Wonder bread wrappers, because they were wax coated, and rub down the slide with those. After the application of a little elbow grease with those, we could literally shoot off the end of the slide at the bottom. The first run down the slide resulted in a very painful butt bump, because I didn't realize I needed to be ready to put my legs down quickly at the end to avoid being dumped off onto my setter.

I had been very impressed with the 1956 Olympics, especially the giant rings event. I had been practicing on our swing set in the backyard, pulling my legs through my arms and hanging backwards, then pulling myself back through the other way, hanging by my knees, and all that.

As I became more proficient with my new mode of transportation, I began to roam a little farther afield. One afternoon as I was riding across the street, between the school buildings, I noticed the iron pipe railings for an outdoor stairway that led down into the school's underground heating facility. I thought to myself, 'self, wouldn't it be great to hang, head down, with arms fully extended, and then pull yourself back up?' I answered myself by getting off the bike, kicking my new kickstand down, and grabbing the top railing. After folding myself at the waist, I pulled my legs up so I was horizontal, then allowed myself to slowly turn from horizontal to vertical, keeping my body straight. My first sign of trouble was when I almost continued over the rail, stopping myself only with more strength in my hands than I knew I had. In spite of that scare, I continued by letting myself down until my arms were fully extended.

At this point, I said to myself, 'self, you really didn't think this all the way through, did you?' The stairwell was at least ten feet deep, and that was pretty hard concrete at the bottom, not soft grass. I tried to pull myself back up, but discovered that I had been a little over optimistic about my strength. I thought about my options: 1) I could just let go, and hope I could get turned over before hitting the ground – NAH!, 2) I could let myself continue to turn over, and then let go and fall feet first to the bottom. That might work, except for the trash at the bottom, and the possibility that my back would bang against the lower rail and concrete wall on the way down, or 3) continue to try to pull myself up. I decided to go with 3,2,1, in that order. I could feel my arms getting very tired, and I knew that if I didn't succeed in pulling myself up on the next try, I would have to resort to option 2. I was beginning to get worried at this point, and maybe that poured more adrenaline into my system, but at any rate, I finally pulled myself back up.

As I stood there catching my breath, I could just hear my mother saying, 'What person in their right mind would do that? (of course, 'right mind' being the operative phrase). You don't have the sense God gave an old goat!' I had to agree with that opinion at this point. I have found in most cases since then, that if I find myself talking to myself, I am usually talking to an idiot.

Of course this latest was no more deranged than some of the other recent stunts I had tried, such as the time I had pulled over half a ton of feed onto myself as I lay on my stomach, to see if that would smash me (it didn't), or the time I had kept climbing to the top of a tree to see if just one more, smaller, limb would hold me (it didn't), or the time I decided to see if it would hurt if I put my hand in the wringer on Mom's washer, like she said (it did), or… well, you get the idea.

Coal Mine Hill

If you travel on Interstate 44 West from St. Louis (which follows the original Route 66), the first rest stop you come to is at the base of Coal Mine Hill. You would never know it today, because there is no sign indicating the land's former use, nor is there any coal lying around. However, in the early 1900's, someone tried to extract some coal from the ground there, but the vein evidently ran out quickly. When I was a kid it was just an ugly scar on the ground between the two lanes of new Route 66, later to become Interstate 44.

The ugly scar became the common trash dump for St. Clair and the surrounding community. People would bring their household trash and dump it in the hole in the ground. Sometime around 1950, there was a great commotion as the St. Clair volunteer fire department was called out. That was no big deal at first, as I was used to the fire siren going off.

We would typically hear that first, then we would hear several cars go roaring by with their vehicle sirens blasting and blue gumballs flashing as the volunteers headed to the fire station. This time though, it was repeated several times during the day (and coming days). As we were to find out later, the trash that had been piled into the shaft at Coal Mine Hill for years had caught fire and was smoking profusely.

My oldest brother, Jerry, went out to see it and said you could see the smoke for miles. It was so thick that Route 66 was closed because you could not see through the dense black cloud. Unfortunately, there was enough coal left in the ground that it caught fire down deep in the hole, and continued to burn for weeks. Fire departments from all over were called out repeatedly, in an effort to put out the conflagration. The fire could not be worked very effectively, because there were no hydrants out that far and the fire was deep in the ground.

For the next several weeks, fire departments would be called out every few days to put down a renewal of the fire. After a while, a decision was made to just let it burn itself out. Large truckloads of big boulders and dirt were hauled in to try to seal up the hole in the hope that it could be starved for oxygen. Eventually it did burn itself out.

In the 1960s, First Lady Ladybird Johnson took on an initiative of Highway Beautification. One of the first pieces of that was the establishment of some rest stops, and the Coal Mine Hill project was one of the first of those. If you stop there today you will notice that the rest stop is in the median, unlike most rest stops that are on either side of the highway. You will also see several of the large boulders that were hauled there.

Meramec Caverns

Meramec Caverns is probably the biggest tourist attraction in our neighborhood. It is part of the same limestone formation that also forms Mammoth Cave in Kentucky. If you travel along I44 today, you cannot avoid seeing signs advertising "Jesse James Hideout" every few miles. Although we lived less than ten miles from the entrance, I had never seen it, so I asked my source for all information about it.

"Roy, have you ever seen Meramec Caverns?"

"Oh, sure, lotsa times. I used to go up there when I was a kid."

"Did you ever see any of Jesse James' loot there, like they say on the signs?"

After considerable laughing, Roy said, "Lester has made a bundle of money on that story, but I don't think there is anything to it. Meramec Caverns was just a small hole in the ground when Jesse James was alive and I really doubt he was ever in it."

"What do you mean, 'a small hole in the ground'?"

"Well, when I was young, the opening into the cave was hardly big enough for one person to get through at a time. In fact, it was not that easy to find. We used to go up there on weekends with some friends and look around with kerosene lanterns, but you couldn't just walk into it. When Mr. Dill bought that land, he blasted the opening like it is today, so he could make a tourist attraction out of it, but back then it was just a small opening in the ground."

"Oh, wow, so you saw Meramec Caverns before it was big like it is today?"

"Yeah, and we would take picnics and stay all day. You could walk around for miles inside, if you had enough kerosene."

The Caverns is located very near the old Route 66, in Stanton, Missouri. Tracks for the St. Louis and San Francisco railroad ran near the highway, and passed through Stanton. One day, travelers were treated to an unusual sight; part of the rail bed had collapsed and left the track appear to be a trestle without a base. Evidently, a part of the Caverns that was not open to the public had collapsed, leaving a giant sinkhole that was visible from the highway. For days, locals were treated to the sight of trucks hauling huge boulders to the area and dumping them into the hole to reestablish the base.

Church

We were in church at least four times every week. Sunday morning we had Sunday School and a church service. Sunday evening we had Training Union (pretty much like Sunday School), then an evening church service. Wednesday evening we had prayer meeting, and small group sessions. The small group sessions for adults were Men's Brotherhood and Women's Missionary Union. For the adolescents we had Royal Ambassadors for the boys and Girls Auxiliary for the girls. On Thursday we had choir practice. As my two older sisters reached their teen-age years they were asked to play the piano and organ for the church services. Then, when my oldest sister, Maxine, got married and moved away I was tapped to play the piano, and later the organ. So that meant I was at the church additional times during the week to practice offertories, preludes, postludes, etc.

Music was a large part of every service, as it was for everyone in our family. My dad was the sole exception in our house. Although he enjoyed music, he had never had the opportunity to learn to play an instrument. His favorite tune was "The Bells of St. Mary's", and he would ask one of us to play it on the piano occasionally. He would mouth the words as we would sing the lyrics. All of us kids played at least one instrument, and we all sang in at least one group; some of us in multiple groups.

Royal Ambassadors

Our Royal Ambassador activities provide the most vivid and pleasant memories for me, as we were very active. This organization provided a great foundation for young men to engage in a Christian atmosphere of learning and fraternity that remains important to me to this day. It was a mixture of Boy Scouts, Indian Guides, Sunday School and Bible Study.

There were ranks within the RA organization that had to be earned. These were Page, Squire, Knight, Ambassador, Ambassador Extraordinary, and Ambassador Plenipotentiary. Each rank required the memorization of some Bible scriptures as well as additional study and activities. Of course, as the ranks increased, the amount and difficulty of these studies and activities increased as well. To be awarded the rank, the boy had to stand a review by a committee of adult men. These were generally picked from among the Men's Brotherhood.

Ranks were awarded at regional meetings of several church groups in the Association, roughly a county-sized group. Once a year, there was a state-wide Royal Ambassador convention in one of the larger cities in Missouri, at which several thousand boys and young men attended.

It was at one of these state conventions that our boys quartet, The Four Deacons were honored to provide the special music. (You're going to hear more about us in the pages following). Backstage, immediately prior to us going out to sing, the music leader for the convention helped us run through our song and gave us some pointers. Other than that, we had no special tutoring or experience. Also, we had no idea about audience interaction. So we marched onto the stage, sang our little song, and marched off.

I have always regretted that we did not have any idea about stage presence. I know our voices blended beautifully, but we did not know how to engage the audience. I feel as though we probably disappointed many people.

Royal Ambassador Chapters were organized in the same fashion as many organizations and groups. We were overseen by a Counselor from the Men's Brotherhood. We elected a President, Vice President, Secretary and Treasurer. Regular meetings were held on Wednesdays before prayer meeting to discuss group activities, progress on rank studies, and other items of interest to the group, as well as general fellowship. We also had fun activities nearly every month. Those activities included swimming, fishing, camping, hayrides, bowling, skating, bonfires, and sometimes we just got together to play lots of games. One of those games involved making each other black out temporarily. We stopped playing that game when one of us fell to the floor and went into a seizure. As he lay there on the floor twitching and thrashing around, we were sure we had killed him. Fortunately for all of us, he recovered in just a few seconds.

On one sunny summer day, a few of us decided to hike down Mill Hill Road, just for fun. We had no particular destination in mind, or specific activity either. We were just hiking. There is a creek that runs down the side of the road, and we decided to hike in the creek bed, which was almost dry at that time of year. We were interested to see what kind of wildlife we could find in the shallow water flowing there. At one point, one of us almost stepped on an alligator snapping turtle as big as a dinner plate. It had dug itself into the creek bed, and its coloring made it almost invisible. All of us jumped when it lunged out of the water at the foot that was about to step on it. After teasing and aggravating it for awhile, we grew tired of that activity and continued down the creek. Due to erosion over the years, the creek bed was about 30 inches deep, so just our shoulders and heads were visible from the fields and road beyond. The creek had wandered away from the road at this point, and there were houses between us in the creek and the road. As we continued our walk, someone came out of the back of their house and yelled something at us; we weren't sure what he was saying. However, the meaning soon became obvious when he produced a shotgun and fired it at us a couple of times. The prairie grass in the field in front of us waved, and a few stalks were blown in our direction as the shot flew around us. We immediately ducked down below the creek bank and beat feet downstream in all haste. And, like the three wise men, we decided to take another way home.

Counselors

This is a good spot for me to pause and pay tribute to the counselors who volunteered their time to guide us into manhood. It was not easy for the church to find people who were willing to give up several of their evenings every month to keep us corralled. I overheard several conversations in which various men were button-holed in an effort to find such a person. And we were ornery enough to give anyone legitimate reasons not to want to volunteer.

Even so, there were several people who stand out in my mind as being very special, and it is only right to give them credit here. They taught us, through example, the meaning and importance of respect for one another, and of giving. Some of those people are mentioned in the following stories.

Cow Patty Ball

Jim Rutledge was in his mid-seventies when he became our counselor. He was not very active, but he knew a lot of people and he was familiar with the area. Jim had a 1953 Pontiac coupe, and took us several places around the countryside where we could let off steam. We usually met at the church and piled into his car, which he then drove to wherever we were to have our special event. In one particular instance, he told us we were going to hunt arrowheads and play softball, so a few of us brought softballs, gloves and a bat or two.

Normally, there would be six to eight kids at any one of these events, but this particular time eleven boys showed up for the game. Jim had nobody to assist him, so all eleven of us piled into his coupe. There were six in the back seat, two in the front seat, and three in the trunk! Jim left the lid open, and we took off from the church with the rear end almost on the ground.

I have no idea where he took us, but it was to a pasture on a hill, and close to a creek. It was a good thing it was not too far because Jim's car needed a new muffler, and fumes were leaking into the back seat as well as into the trunk. We kept the windows down, but the fumes seemed to sweep into the trunk and hang there. In addition, dust from the dry gravel roads we had traveled to get to our playground had blown into the trunk during the entire trip and coated each of the three occupants to a medium brown. Because it was also hot, and there was considerable sweat involved, the three looked like walking mud pies. After shaking out shirts, they were turned inside out, and used to wipe off faces and arms.

This was hardly a regulation ball diamond. We were on top of a hilly pasture that sloped away to the creek, and was covered with Queen Anne's Lace, dandelions, timothy, alfalfa, crabgrass, and all manner of other weeds. The cattle that had been occupying the pasture provided our bases – cow patties. So, we played cow patty softball for a while, until we grew hot and tired. Then we adjourned to the creek to swim in our underwear and look for arrowheads.

I wish I knew where that place was. There were arrowheads every-where. All of us came back with several of them. I had at least a dozen, and I think everyone else had a similar number. Jim brought us back home and dumped out a rather filthy, sweaty, muddy pile of stinky boys on the church property. We were exhausted, but we had a wonderful time.

Jim was very patient with us, and I will always remember his kind face and ready smile. He had a great sense of humor, and a good sense of how far to let us go before tugging on the leash. He was never cross with us, and his Christian compassion was there for all to see. He did not wear his faith on his sleeve as some do, but his example was clear as glass.

Camping

The St. Louis and San Francisco Railroad ran through St. Clair, and across the back line of our property. Nearly all the old steam locomotives had been retired in favor of the new diesel/electric ones, but I recall one or two of the old steamers going by when I was very young. The sound of the old steam engines was distinctly different from the rumble of the diesel engines, so it was easy to tell when an old one came by.

There was a small depot in St. Clair, which looked very much like those you can see in any old Western movie. The station master was a rather short, round elf of a man, who would have made an ideal Santa Claus. He always had a ready laugh and a pleasant word for everyone. I rode with Dad several times when he took boxes of newly hatched chickens to the station for shipment to other parts of the country, or to pick up supplies that had been shipped to us.

Doren Creswell retired from his job as station master and agreed to become our RA counselor. That was the start of a series of events that would affect the life of the whole church for well over two decades. Mr. Creswell was not a rich man. He lived in a bungalow situated on about twenty acres that was bordered on the back side by the Little Meramec River, about seven miles outside of town. Most of the twenty or so acres was in pasture land, but a strip about 100 feet wide next to the river had been eroded into a bottom about ten feet below the level of the pasture. The river itself was spring-fed and gravel-bottomed, and ran perfectly clear and cold. It flowed directly at the property along the property line, then made a right-angle turn to flow along the back of the property. The cause of this was the rocky bluff on the other side of the river. These limestone bluffs are very common in Missouri, and always create a very scenic landscape. Those bluffs rose up across the stream about 80 feet above the water. Since the stream came crashing into the property at right angles before being forced to change direction, the deepest part of the stream was on the near bank, as any river rat or canoeist could have predicted. Then the river became shallower toward the far bank, disappearing into a sand bar that was submerged during spring runoffs.

This property gave Doren the ideal location to let loose a bunch of hooligans where they couldn't do much harm. Our first few outings there were afternoon fishing trips; the river bottom was covered with fish. In these fast-running, cold waters, there were mostly bluegill, redear, rock bass and suckers, with some largemouth bass and channel catfish as well. After a few of the outings just for fishing and softball, we began staying into the evening, before Doren or his daughter would drive us back into town. Eventually, he agreed to allow us to camp overnight. This involved a certain amount of trust, because there would be campfires and no supervision of the tribe for several hours.

He came down to the campsite (the bottom) after dark to check on the placement of the fire and to suggest that we needed to remain on his property. (He didn't say, but he may have received some calls from his neighbors asking about all those loud idiots wading up and down the creek.) To our surprise, he brought his harmonica. None of us knew he even had one, much less knew how to play it. He played for quite a while, and we sang along. "Camptown Races", "She'll Be Comin' Round the Mountain", "Arkansas Traveler", "Goober Peas" and lots of other old tunes. He played Chattanooga Choo-Choo and several other tunes I did not know, and we had a great time for over an hour. Then, after he checked everything over he went back to the house and left us for the evening. By that time we were totally exhausted, because other than fish, we had played softball in the pasture, swam for a while, chopped and gathered wood for the fire, and cleaned up our dishes after fixing our dinner. Of course, we had had a very balanced meal of hot dogs and marshmallows, washed down with gallons of apple cider.

This was so much fun that it became the normal activity for our meetings. In fact, for a few years we camped there year-round. Winter camping was just as popular as summer camping. Sure it was cold, but there were no mosquitoes to bother us. One drawback to winter camping for us was that none of us had any winter gear, other than regular winter coats. Consequently, the campfire became all the more important.

One January, we camped there when it had been cold enough for several days to partially freeze over the spring-fed Little Meramec. Even though it was cold there was no snow on the ground yet, so it was dry. We set up our tents (I had an Army surplus shelter half), and began to gather firewood for the all-important campfire. Once that was done, we began to explore around the campsite to see what we could do for that evening and the next day.

Fishing always seemed to be a part of our camping trips, but on this occasion, the river was partially frozen over. Vernon decided that would be no problem, because he would just poke a hole in the ice and do some ice fishing. He found a broken tree limb with a jagged and somewhat pointed end, and began pounding at the ice. Unfortunately, he neglected to consider that he should be standing on the shore side of the hole he was pounding, and when the hole was pounded all the way through, it continued as cracks in all directions. The ice broke away, and Vernon fell into the freezing water.

After we recovered from our hysterical laughing fits, we realized that we should be helping him get out of the water, so we found more branches and extended them to him so he could grab hold and pull himself out. Not being the most expert campers, most of us had not thought to bring along changes of clothes, so Vernon was not able to change into dry clothes. Fortunately, Doren had decided to check on us and immediately went back to his house and brought some of his clothes for Vernon to change into.

Now, Doren weighed over 300 pounds, stood about 5-feet, 5-inches tall, and must have had about a 55-inch waist. Vernon stuck both of his legs into one leg of Doren's pants, and wrapped the other one around himself, then tied that on with some rope. The legs were big enough that he still had room to take small to medium steps in the one leg. He had to wear that for the rest of the night until his pants dried in front of the fire.

The limestone bluffs across the river were almost always dripping water from the hill above, and of course with the temperature at well below freezing, icicles formed as the water came to the surface. The next morning we were looking at those icicles, and decided to have a contest to see which one of us could bring the largest one back to camp. Of course, since the bluffs came right to the water's edge that meant we had to wade the creek to retrieve the icicles. Remembering Vernon, most of us decided to wade the creek in our underwear, so we would have some dry pants to put on after the contest ended. (Remember, this is January!)

All of us made several trips across and then up the creek to retrieve the largest icicle we could carry. It was tricky to try to knock the icicles loose without breaking them, or allowing them to fall into the river (or on our heads!). After a trip to the bluffs, we would stand as close to the fire as we dared to warm ourselves. Whenever someone would set a new record, the whole gang would redeploy along the bluffs to try to bring home a larger one. Looking back, I can't believe that none of us suffered hypothermia, or came down with colds or pneumonia.

In the end, it was David Armstrong who brought in the largest icicle, weighing well over 100 pounds, I'm sure. Before the end of it broke off it had been about ten feet long, and it was about 18 inches across at the base. I don't think any of the rest of us could have carried it back.

In the spring, eight or ten of us were back for another camping trip, and decided to camp on the sandbar that had formed in the middle of the creek, right in front of our normal campsite. After our normal clowning around and much foolishness, we bedded down for the night with our makeshift beds circling the campfire. Somebody woke in the middle of the night because his bedroll was wet. There must have been some rain upstream from us, and the creek had risen about 18 inches. We were almost completely surrounded by water and it was rising quickly. We all grabbed our bedrolls and other gear and waded back across the cold, fast-flowing channel to our normal campsite, which was somewhat higher. By morning, the sandbar was completely covered. So much for camping on the sandbar.

After a year or so of us having this wonderful, idyllic place to ourselves, Mr. Creswell decided to donate the bottom land next to the creek to the church, and the church decided to build a lodge on it for church gatherings. The land was dedicated by the church as Creswell Baptist Park. Several men of the church donated their time to build the lodge, and it was put up in just a few weeks one summer. The lodge was built like many riverside buildings in the area, on pilings about fourteen feet above ground level to keep it out of flood waters. The building was about thirty feet by sixty feet, and included a complete kitchen, but no fireplace and no provision for heat.

The building did serve to extend the number of nights we could comfortably camp there, since we could go inside if it was raining or snowing. However, it had been situated on what had been our campsite, and somehow it didn't have the same remote feeling as when we were out there 'all alone'. Consequently, we gradually made less and less use of it for that purpose, although the church did have many great all-church picnics and outings there.

Merle Wilson was another counselor who donated a lot of his time to us. His son, Chuck, was in our RA group and we had a lot of fun together. One weekend, Mr. Wilson took us camping at Meramec State Park about twelve miles west of St. Clair, south of Sullivan, Missouri. This was after the lodge had been built at Creswell Baptist Park.

We set up our tents and roasted hot dogs for dinner, then set out exploring. Fisher Cave was very close and we looked through that, then went swimming. After that, we began playing some touch football. There happened to be a full moon that evening, so we played long after dark. I was really amazed that we could easily see the football so late at night. Fortunately, there were not many people in the park (we didn't see any), because we played and made lots of noise until long after midnight.

Music

My mother loved music, and made sure all of us had the opportunity to participate in all the musical culture and events available in our area. She had worked as a domestic employee from the age of 9 to save up for a piano, and wanted all of us to be able to play some instrument.

Out of six children only Jerry, the oldest, did not take lessons and learn to play the piano. All of us though, played in the school band, and we all sang in the church choir and in various small groups. My road to stardom began as a five-year-old in the Beginners Sunday School Class at church, when we were to perform a special number for the church congregation. Our director, Mrs. Monte, played the introduction to "Jesus Loves Me" twice, and nobody sang – we just stood there, frozen in front of all those people. Finally, I started singing by myself, and finished the song pretty much as a solo, to the delight of the entire church, who were laughing heartily at our predicament.

Tickling the Ivories

Mother signed me up to take piano lessons from a lady named Lillian Crawford. Mrs. Crawford lived in St. Louis, and came out to St. Clair a few days a week on the bus to teach a few of us ruffians some culture. She was a very nice lady but often became very upset with me, because I hated to practice and usually came to a lesson totally unprepared.

Much of our effort was in preparation for a competition in St. Louis, in which we would be judged and receive a pin if we did well enough. These competitions were usually located in a large piano factory in St. Louis, but one time we put on a rather ambitious concert at the Scottish Rites Temple, in which there were many individual performances and then a gigantic duet piece, with over fifty pianos playing (somewhat) together.

As I grew older, I continued piano lessons with another lady who had played the scores for silent movies. As she told it, the piano was located down front, in what might be called the orchestra pit, except that she was the only musician. She was given the score that went with a particular movie, and had to synchronize her playing with what was happening on the screen. It was very common for the film to break during the show, but the music was not to stop. She had to continue playing extemporaneously while the technician repaired the film. Then the movie would restart, unannounced, and she was expected to continue playing and pick up with wherever the movie was at that point. Sometimes the technician would roll the movie forward several frames, and sometimes backward several frames.

She had a beautiful concert grand piano in her home that took up the entire parlor. Gail and I went to her house a couple of times to visit, but mostly just to hear her play. It was amazing to me that you could ask her to play almost anything, any genre, and mood, and she could just start playing and go on for as long as you wanted to listen.

The Four Deacons

Mother conspired with a couple of other mothers in church to have four of us to form a quartet, for the purpose of providing special music at some church services. It seems that she was on familiar ground because my older brother had also sung in a quartet for a time, and both my older sisters had sung in trios and quartets as well. I loved singing, and launched into it with both lungs. As I look back on that time, I realize that I did not so much hunger for the performance or the applause as some performers do. I have heard several professional singers attest that the audience reaction is what they yearn for, and that there is quite an ego boost that comes with the applause and praise. Not so for me. First of all, we lived in a time and place where church music was not applauded. That would have been sacrilege!! No, in the First Baptist Church, the most response one could expect might be an occasional isolated, quiet 'Amen'. No hands in the air, no applause, no yelling, no standing – maybe some smiles.

No, what I really appreciate about that time is the friendship we developed as four friends having a really good time. We had no professional advice or training, but we came together to practice for a couple of hours at a time, usually several times a week. When we performed together the ride to and from the venue was consumed with singing. Not practicing our numbers for the performance, but just fun gospel and nonsense songs that we loved to sing together. I loved the process of creating harmony with my three buddies.

Over time we were asked to sing in more and more places, and eventually came to realize that it would be convenient if we had a name. It was always awkward for people to ask for us as "…that group of boys from St. Clair, you know, at the church – First Baptist – who is in it now?" At that time, the full extent of creativeness in group naming consisted of the article 'the', usually a number, and a noun, as in The Four Seasons, The Four Tops, The Lettermen, The Four Freshmen, The Righteous Brothers, etc. So, we followed convention, not being very creative ourselves, and became The Four Deacons. We weren't even very creative in the names of the participants; we had two Garys and two Duanes (although my name is spelled differently). Even funnier, when the oldest Gary graduated from high school and moved away to attend college, we replaced him with another Gary.

We sang at our own church of course, often providing the special music for Sunday morning or evening services. We also sang at school functions, service club meetings, and lots of other venues. One of our local musicians, Ken Capehart, was a guitar player who sang gospel music around the area, and had a spot on the local radio station, KLPW, every Sunday morning at 8 AM. He honored us by asking us to sing backup for him on that spot. There were no rehearsals; we all knew the songs. We were to provide harmony as he sang the lead. We did not have headphones as performers do today, and no provision for feedback so we could tell how we were sounding. We did not want to overwhelm his voice so we sang softly, as we would for a live spot. However, with him singing directly into the microphone and us in back of him, nobody at home could hear us at all. I assume he received some comments to the effect that he announced us every week, but nobody could hear us. All I know is that, after a short time, we were simply not asked to return.

On the other hand, someone from the state Baptist organization heard us sing, and recruited us to sing at the state convention of Royal Ambassadors. What an honor that was for us! We appeared in front of several thousand boys and men to sing one song. That was our two minutes of fame.

Band

My oldest brother, Jerry, had played clarinet in the high school band. My two older sisters had played in the band. So, when I became old enough it only seemed right that I should also play in the band. Since Jerry had graduated already, I inherited his clarinet, which was fortunate because by this time my parents weren't doing so well economically and there was no money for another musical instrument. Mr. Wright, the band instructor, started a beginners' class in late summer before school started. This was to become the junior high band and I was in sixth grade. The band included sixth, seventh and eighth grade students. By the time school started a few weeks later, we beginners could at least understand what Mr. Wright was talking about, and play a few notes.

Jerry's clarinet was a single-piece metal instrument that was different from everyone else's. All the others were the black, multi-piece wooden instruments most of us recognize. I felt odd and somewhat embarrassed because my clarinet was different from the others. It's amazing how this kind of thing can create pressure in people – especially young people. Fortunately for me, nobody made fun of me or my clarinet so I just slinked into my chair and played the music.

One issue that did develop was that I did not play first chair, and my mother wanted to know why. My mother knew that I was playing the music as well or better than any of the other players and she was involved enough to ask Mr. Wright about it. She was respectful about it; she merely asked the question. Mr. Wright explained that yes, I was probably the best player in the band, especially considering that I was just a beginner, but that the metal clarinet did not have the same sound quality as the wooden instruments and he could not put me into first chair with the shiny silver metal clarinet. Mother accepted the explanation but began saving money, and a year later I had a new clarinet, black, shiny and wooden like all the rest. I was promoted to first chair for the Junior High Band.

In our school system at this time, High School was four years; ninth through twelfth grades. So, when I was old enough to be in the High School band, I started at the back, as one might suspect. I believe we had sixteen clarinets, and I was in the fourth row. By the time I was a Junior though, I was promoted to first chair again. In a larger school, I probably would have been stuck in the back row because I hated to practice and was really not that good.

Our band was not that active; we played at halftime during basketball games (we did not have football), and marched in a couple of local parades (Homecoming and Halloween) during the year. We played two concerts during the year and went to the state music contest, and that was about it.

Being part of the Band program meant that there was no time for other elective classes, so a decision had to be made that Band is where one wanted to be. In addition to Band, I was also involved in the High School Chorus and Boy's Glee Club. Although my activities with the Four Deacons meant some school-related performances, we practiced outside of school and received no credit for that. As with the Four Deacons, I thoroughly enjoyed the camaraderie in the bands and singing groups. Many friendships developed there that have been permanent, and that I cherish.

Warm Summer Nights

When I was younger my older sisters, Maxine and Janet, were the church organist and pianist, respectively. In those days those were unpaid positions. When Maxine moved on to college, then got married in 1958, I was asked to take her place. I had never played the organ, so had to take a few lessons to learn about all the stops and foot pedals.

On Sunday evenings, especially in the summer, we often wouldn't have two musicians, so I played the piano for the services. After the initial singing and offering, I would move from the piano bench to the front pew while the minister gave the sermon. As he wound up the sermon, he would always say some concluding remark like, '…now, as we come to the close of the service…', and that was my cue to move back to the piano and begin playing introductory bars to the closing hymn.

One particularly hot summer evening I could not stay awake, and finally succumbed to slumber. As the minister gave my cue to move, I didn't, so he said the same words again, and still I didn't move. He tried a different set of concluding remarks with similar results. I finally woke as he was saying, "Would somebody please wake the pianist?" I was so embarrassed I wanted to crawl under the pew and disappear. After the service I got a lot of good-natured ribbing, even from the pastor.

Summer Camp

The Franklin County Baptist Association owned a property at Spring Bluff that was used mostly for summer camps and retreats. Summer camp sessions were five days long, Monday through Friday. There were two sessions for boys (younger and older) and two for girls. The camp had progressed to the point that we had concrete block bunk houses. The houses were constructed wide enough to include a row of bunkbeds along each wall, with a central aisle along the length of the building. The bunk beds were made of 2x4s, with chicken wire stretched over them to form the base for whatever bedding we brought. There were daily Bible studies and worship services, mixed with lots of great activities such as softball, swimming, pillow fights, skits, bonfires, etc.

At the end of the senior boys week there was usually a Friday evening retreat for adult men (the Brotherhood), which involved a meal Friday evening, a vespers service, overnight stay, breakfast on Saturday and a morning service in the outdoor chapel, which was just a crude open-sided shelter with plank benches. One year my best friend, Gary, and I were asked to stay over after our week and help serve dinner to the men's group Friday evening. We were assured that someone would inform our parents that we would not be home until Saturday morning. Since camp ended at noon on Friday, we would have the entire afternoon to do as we pleased. It was an offer we couldn't refuse.

As soon as lunch had been served everyone packed up and found their rides home, leaving Gary and I all alone – I mean, ALL alone. No adult supervision! We hightailed it back to our bunks, changed into our swimming trunks and ran to the CONCRETE swimming pool. (All of our swimming was done in creeks and rivers. There were no swimming pools in our area.) We were sure we would have to climb the six-foot fence, but the gate had been left unlocked, so we just waltzed in like we owned the place and swam for the next four – yep, FOUR hours.

Around 5PM we decided we should shower and change to be ready for our jobs at the dinner. It was only then that we realized just how tired and sunburned we were. We both looked like overdone lobsters, and had about as much starch left in our bodies as a wet rag. By the end of the evening we were both nearly walking in our sleep as we served and then bussed the tables. Neither of us had any trouble sleeping that night.

Hayrides

A couple of times each year one of the farmers in the church would volunteer to pull his wagon, lined with haybales, to the church and the RAs would go on a hayride. Typically, the wagon would arrive around dusk, and the kids would begin to gather around it and take up their favorite spots on it as more people came. After everyone was aboard we would take off down the street, pass through the middle of town and usually head down Mill Hill Road. St. Clair was so small that the in-town ride was only about five minutes long before we were in the country on gravel roads.

It was so much fun to listen to the big old single-cylinder John Deere putt-putting along the road through the silent evening, watching the stars become brighter, and sitting next to my date for the evening. The first hayride of the year happened to occur at the middle of August, during the height of the Perseid meteor shower (although I didn't know it at the time – had never heard of it), and the 'shooting stars' were plentiful and bright. My date allowed me to put my arm around her waist as we sat there and were awed by the sight. It felt so sweet!

Somewhere on the ride the tractor stopped and we hiked a short distance to a spring that flowed clear and cold out of a limestone bluff. Then the wagon climbed for a while, and we were treated to the sight of Lost Hill, a knob that rose out of the flat Meramec River bottom. The gravel road climbed about halfway up the hill and made a hairpin turn around the narrow peak to return down the other side. As we climbed the hill, we could see cars that had tried to take the curve too fast and had ended up perched in the tops of huge Sycamores.

The halfway point involved a stop at someone's house where we had hotdogs and marshmallows over a campfire. Then we remounted the wagon for the ride home. These were my first experiences of events involving a 'date' of sorts, as boys and girls paired up under adult, responsible supervision. I think it gave me a good foundation for respectful relationships.

Salvation

We were Southern Baptist. As I mentioned before, that may have been a matter of convenience as the church was across the street and down only a couple of lots from us. My father had been brought up in the Champion City Church, which was Methodist, but Mom had been baptized Presbyterian, I believe. Anyway, in that church there is a strong belief in the requirement to publicly repent of one's sins and confess belief in Jesus Christ to receive salvation.

At the end of every worship service there is an altar call, or Invitation, to come down to the front of the church, to the altar, and publicly indicate this action. Those feeling the call of God respond by leaving their seats and making the journey to the altar. This can be a very emotional experience, and in itself contains a strong cleansing, or cathartic, effect. The minister assists each individual in working through the emotions of reaching this momentous decision, and helping to engender a feeling of relief and happiness that this step has been taken.

At the very end of the service, the minister usually asked the supplicant(s) to stand with him, and then announced what had transpired. In many cases this was a general confession of sinfulness and a plea for salvation. For many who felt they had 'backslid', it may have been an announcement of rededication of their vows to follow God, and in some cases also a request for rebaptism as a further step to solidify their relationship to God.

I was nine years old when I accepted Jesus Christ as my Savior. We were worshipping in the ground level of the new educational wing because the sanctuary was being remodeled and enlarged. It was 1954. I had been in the church all my life, and was familiar with at least the rudiments and outward steps involved in salvation. It was generally recognized in our congregation that people were somewhat protected from damnation until they reached the 'age of accountability', which was loosely thought of as age nine or so. At that point, it was felt that children had developed a good, if not complete, sense of right and wrong. Mother began asking me if I felt the need to 'step forward' and take that leap into salvation. Finally I did so, and went through that experience. I believe Reverend Holly was our minister then.

Our church did not have a baptistry at the time, although one was being added as part of the remodeling. Consequently, baptisms were conducted in the river; the Meramec River, to be specific. Since it was a big deal to have the whole congregation meet at a remote location, baptisms were held infrequently; once or twice a year. Everyone who had made 'the walk' since the last baptism service stood in line to perform the ritual of death, burial and resurrection anew in Christ that baptism signified. The minister would wade into the water to about midstream, say a few words about the decisions that had been made by those in line, and what those decisions signified in terms of being a Christian, and then the newly-faithful would be invited to advance into the river to be baptized. The river was spring fed, and was always cold, even in the summer. So, when I was baptized in April, it was REALLY cold.

The whole church gathered on the gravelly banks of the river on a bright spring Sunday. We sang songs including, I think, "Shall We Gather At The River", "Amazing Grace", and "I Surrender All", and the baptism candidates lined up single file down into the river, where the minister stood in his wool baptism suit and waders. I was one of about twenty or thirty candidates that day, and stood at the back of the line.

The closer I got to the front of the line, the cloudier it got. I reached the minister, he raised his right hand and cradled my neck with his left and pronounced the blessing on me. Then his right hand, holding a handkerchief, was placed over my nose and I was lowered into the 'grave' of the cleansing water, then raised up again. As I waded back to shore, soaking wet and shivering, the sky opened up and the wind started to blow. Lightning flashed across the sky and thunder roared overhead louder than a cannon. Rain began falling in huge drops, and so thick it was as if it were poured from a bucket. People scrambled for their cars; the minister 'ran on water' to get out before lightning got him. Mom threw a towel around me and we beat feet for the car.

We dispensed with the closing prayer and songs. The service was over.

Over the years I have made fun of the circumstances surrounding my baptism and the "omen", but I wonder...

Evidently, God still has something for me to do because I'm still around, but I try to be really, really careful.

The Hawk

Glenn lived a few miles west of us, just off of Springfield Road, the same street that I lived on. When the city limit was reached, it became a 'road' instead of an 'avenue'. The 'avenue' was paved, but became gravel at the city limit. I occasionally walked out to his house to hang out. We usually hiked through the fields and pastures around there just looking at things, and discovering all kinds of neat stuff.

One day we stumbled onto an old cow carcass. It had been there a long time; there was no meat or hide left and the bones were bleached white. The scavengers had done a good job of cleaning up. I don't know why, but I decided it would be a great thing to have a tooth from the old cow so I knocked a molar out of the skull with a rock and put it in my pocket. It would have been neater to have the whole skull, but we were going to be out all day, and I didn't want to carry that thing around.

Much later I decided it would look great to wear that thing around my neck, like an Indian (like an Indian would be proud to wear a cow's tooth!). I drilled a hole in the tooth, and strung a long lamp pull chain through it. Now I had something cool to wear to school! It's a good thing my mom never saw me off to school – she would have been mortified. But I digress.

As we were walking through a pasture, we came upon a lone large Oak tree with a hawk nest in the top. Glenn climbed up to see if the nest was occupied. Sure enough, there were three eggs in the nest. He climbed back down and we talked about those eggs for quite a while as we continued walking. The conversation gradually turned to falconry, and we began to wonder if we could train a hawk to be a trained hunter. I began to visualize myself as a medieval knight wearing a thick leather gauntlet, and having this falcon fly away and return to my arm at my beck and call. Really heady stuff.

I began to wonder how one goes about training a hawk to be a falcon. We didn't have the internet in those days; heck, we didn't have computers! So, if one wanted some information on a given topic one would consult one's copy of the Encyclopedia Britannica, or Colliers' Encyclopedia, or whatever brand one had. So I picked out the F volume of our Collier's, and found there was not much on the topic that would be of any help. The next step was our local library, which also had nothing on the topic. However, the librarian was very helpful and informed me she could order information from some larger library database somewhere. So I put in my request and in a couple of weeks she called to let me know she had a few photocopied (thermofaxed) pages of information for me. Yeah, it was a couple of weeks, not a few nanoseconds. And it was a few pages, not ten million hits from the cloud (which we thought contained rain, not information).

In a few weeks we went back to the tree and Glenn again climbed up the tree to see if the babies were ready to be plucked from the nest. They were pretty much fledged out, so it was time. Otherwise it would be too late – both because they would have left the nest, and because to raise a falcon, we learned we needed to get them imprinted on us from the earliest age possible.

The rest of us remained on the ground standing around the tree. Buck had his trusty .22 semiauto rifle, in case Momma came back while Glenn was up there in the top of the tree. In fact, it wasn't long before she returned and began screeching and divebombing Glenn as he robbed the nest. Buck dutifully sprayed several rounds in the air around the tree to drive her away (what, you don't think that was dangerous, with Glenn up there do you?!). As he grabbed the last fledgling Glenn hastily retreated back down the tree as fast as he could, and we ran away with our prize of purloined predatory poultry – our find of filched feathered future falconry (sorry, I couldn't help myself).

I bought some leather gloves to use as a gauntlet to carry and receive my returning falcon, in readiness for our first hunt together. I also made some leather thongs from boot strings to attach to the falcon's legs.

We had a root cellar room in the basement under the back porch, and I put cardboard over the windows to create a cave-like darkness. That was one of the first things suggested in the article I had obtained. After a few days in the dark, I began to visit my new predator with more frequency, and to give it a little more light and feed it.

In two weeks I moved my hunter to a pen Dad had built to raise turkeys. It had wire sides, a slat floor, a roosting space and about seven feet of headroom. It was about twenty feet square, so it offered some room for the bird to maneuver around freely, so I didn't have to keep it tethered. After about a month, I felt the bird was imprinted on me enough that I could take it out of the cage and show it off. I opened the door and offered up my gauntleted arm. He (or she, how did I know) immediately left its perch and flew to my arm. I was ecstatic! Of course, it helped that I was holding a small chunk of meat in my fist.

I carried my prize, purloined pin-feathered predator to the house to show it to the rest of the family. Mom was less than thrilled but was really gratified that it was not a skunk, or a rabbit that would soon turn into thousands. (Maybe the second son had a little more promise.)

I worked with that bird for several weeks, and it would come at my call. However, I never got to see if I could train it to hunt because, tragically, it died. As I think back on that episode now, I feel guilt at having robbed nature of a beautiful thing for my own pleasure. Although we didn't have any thoughts of conservation back then, and didn't realize we were doing anything wrong, I see now that there are reasons why there are laws against people trying to keep wild animals; for their protection.

DeWayne showing off the red-tailed hawk in our living room

Wild River

One of the more beautiful natural features in central Missouri is the Meramec River. This river literally 'springs' out of Meramec Springs, located south of St. James. The huge spring is one of several that breach the surface in a generally north-south direction along Highway 19 south of Route 66. These springs are the result of the limestone bedrock underlying the surface soil of much of the Midwest, left over from our ancient history when most of central North America was an inland sea, and is part of the same formation that extends down into Kentucky, and forms Mammoth Cave. Meramec River meanders through east central and southeast Missouri, finally emptying into the mighty Mississippi River south of St. Louis. Because it is spring-fed, including several spring-fed tributaries, the river is generally cold most of the year. Also due to its underlying bed of porous limestone, sinkholes occasionally open up in unexpected places, causing whirlpools and undertows that claim lives every year. These transient sinkholes also produce some deep water where lunker fish lurk. Consequently, anglers are lured back to the river time after time for big fish, and some do not come home. It seemed that everyone I knew had been touched by a death on the river. Either a family member, close acquaintance or someone else they knew of had been lost to them.

High School

had never been one to think much about the significance of events in my life. Many things came easy for me, and those that did not I shrugged off and let go. I had tried out for the basketball team but was not good enough to make the varsity team. Coach Sullivan had allowed me to suit up with the B team as a Sophomore, but it was soon very obvious that I was never going to make the grade. I just didn't have the eye-hand coordination to be a good player. Even though I played a few minutes in a couple of games, I quit toward the end of the season. I was somewhat disappointed, but not overly so, and I moved onto other things. One of the advantages of going to a small school was that there were lots of opportunities to participate, even for mediocre performers like me.

In fact, my dilemma was not what I could do, but how to work in everything that I was doing. As a high school student, I participated in nearly everything the school had to offer. I was in the concert band, which was also the marching band. I had moved up to first chair in the clarinet section with very little effort. I mention that not in a bragging way, but to say that I could have been much better if I had devoted even a modicum of effort to practice. The problem was always time. A few of us had also tried to work up a small combo we called a stage band, although that didn't go anywhere. Then there was glee club and boys' chorus.

After showing almost no skills for basketball, I tried out for the track team. Fortunately, I was good enough to participate in the 100-yard and 220-yard sprints, as well as two relay teams. Coach wanted me to try hurdles, but I had no interest in that. Our school had a cinder track at the time, and I had seen what hurdlers looked like after tangling with a hurdle during a race. It was bloody and painful.

On the academic side, I took every elective I could work in, so that I never had a study hall or empty spot on my schedule. Here again, I didn't really apply myself. I did homework only when necessary and rarely studied beyond that absolutely required to keep up in class. Fortunately for me, that was enough so that I was always on the honor roll, and was elected to the National Junior Honor Society, and then the National Honor Society.

In fact, my election to the National Honor Society was the source of yet another disappointment for one of my teachers who wanted so much for me to perform better. Miss MacKenzie was the school librarian and a personal friend of my mother's. They were always discussing what should be done about my laziness with regard to my studies. She rarely missed an opportunity to gently scold me about my less than stellar performance.

On the day that the Society appointments were announced, all those elected were assembled on stage in the gymnasium for a group photograph to be published in the school and local papers. That day happened to be one of several when one of the feeder calves I was raising got out, and I had to chase it down, get it back to the pasture, locate the place where it had escaped, and repair the fence. By the time I got to school, the group was already gathering onstage, and people were looking for me.

As usual, I had no idea about the election or the photographs, so I was surprised when a teacher found me and told me to hotfoot it to the gym. Miss MacKenzie was already getting the group lined up for the photograph and was horrified when she turned and saw my approach. I had not had time to change, so I still had on my muddy boots, my bluejeans were covered with mud and manure, and I smelled of sweat and cow dung. She hustled me to the back of the group so that only my head was visible. Needless to say, there were many snickers among the group and a very distraught Miss MacKenzie.

Outside of school, I participated in many activities among which I had to divide my time. Royal Ambassadors met every Wednesday, and we also had occasional outings like hayrides, fishing and camping trips, conventions, etc, that required extra time. I sang in the choir, which practiced on Thursday, until I was named as church pianist, then organist, which required me to practice several times a week, in addition to practicing with the choir. Our quartet, The Four Deacons, practiced often, and sang at various events regularly, in churches, schools, service club meetings, etc. Since I was the church organist, I would often be tapped to play for funerals. Once in a great while, someone would be generous enough to give me five dollars for playing, but mostly I did it for nothing. I was even allowed to leave school for these funerals. In the summer, I also played on the church softball team, which involved practices, and games usually on Friday or Saturday night. And lastly, I tried for a while to participate in Explorer Scouts, although that did not last very long; I had finally reached saturation and had to give up something.

Taum Sauk Trail

"Glenn, I think I am going to quit Explorers. I just don't have time for everything, and need to drop something. Explorers is the newest thing for me, and I really haven't gotten into all of it anyway, so I think that is the thing I should get out of."

"Well, I wish you wouldn't quit, but I understand. But at least stay in for a few more weeks. We're going to go on a hike before school starts up again."

"Oh, really? Where are we going?"

"We're going to hike over Taum Sauk Mountain."

"Oh, man, that would be fun! I'm in. I'll stay with the group at least until after that, then I'll see."

Taum Sauk is the highest mountain in Missouri, at 1,772 feet. It is part of the St. Francois range, and is skirted by the St. Francis River, in Iron County. Unlike many mountains in North America that were formed by tectonic uplift, much of the St. Francois range was formed volcanically, so the area is rich in minerals like iron, lead and granite.

For the next couple of weeks I busied myself collecting what I would need for a long hike and overnight camping trip. Bob Schuler, my future brother-in-law, had provided me with some army surplus castoffs from his time as a ROTC cadet, so I had a pair of used combat boots, a canteen with a web belt to clip it on, a pup tent and a duffel bag. I scrounged a couple of burlap sacks and plastic sheeting to use as a ground cloth and bought four pairs of boot socks. I was ready.

On the appointed day, I rose long before sunup, put on my tee shirt, bluejeans, bootsocks and combat boots. I swung the loaded duffel bag over my shoulder and walked the mile or so to the American Legion post where we were all meeting. I threw my gear onto the stake truck with everyone else's, and climbed up onto the flat bed of the truck.

At 5AM the truck began its 60-mile journey with a dozen or so Explorer Scouts and all of our gear for an overnight camping and hiking adventure. The trail began at Elephant Rocks, which I had seen once before as a younger child. It is a strange jumble of pink granite boulders, some as high as a two-story building, seemingly thrown about by some mystical giant. It is surrounded by a dense, oak-hickory forest so typical of Missouri.

We arrived at the park about 6:30AM and dismounted, ready to conquer the trail. However, our adult leader quickly dampened our enthusiasm.

"We have to wait for the guide, boys."

"Guide?! We don't need any guide! We're country boys; we know how to find our way through the woods."

"Sorry, guys – that's the rule." Anybody taking the trail has to have an experienced guide to lead them."

"Oh, man! When is he going to get here?"

"Well, he's supposed to be here before 7 O'Clock."

"Who is he? Do we know him?"

"He's an Eagle Scout, and I'm sure you don't know him."

Glenn was an Eagle Scout, but except for him, none of the rest of us had even been in scouting earlier, so there was considerable disdain of the kind only Missouri rednecks like us could generate.

"Where is he from?" In our minds, it might have been ok if this so-called guide had been from St. Clair, Union, Lonedell, or one of the other local communities known to us.

"He's from St. Louis." Our adult counselor had only been reluctantly feeding us answers to our questions and not being terribly forthcoming, because he knew what our reactions were going to be.

"St. Louis?! An Eagle Scout!? This is too much. We have to wait on a smart-alec Eagle shit from St. Louis?!"

"Yeah, I'm afraid that's about the size of it, and there's no point complaining any more about it. It won't be so bad; he's probably a really nice guy."

On the way down in the truck, we had been wondering what the record was for completing the trail. Most of us were on the high school cross country and track teams, and records were things we always thought about. We were confident we could complete the trail in record time and have some extra time to swim at Johnson's Shut-Ins. Having to put up with a guide was going to seriously hamper our style and having to have one who was a dandy from St. Louis was even more insulting to us.

Seven O'Clock came and went. Eight O'Clock passed us by. Seven other groups of scouts arrived and started down the trail.

"Hey, why are those other groups allowed to start the trail?"

"Because they have their guides with them."

"Hey, how about us just tagging along behind them then? We would be following a guide."

"No, we can't do that, because our guide is already on his way."

"Well, where is he then?"

"Look, I don't know any more than you do about that. Now just be quiet and sit down there by the truck until he gets here."

We realized we were being a bunch of snots, so we shut up and explored the rocky area of giant boulders. That passed the time, and we were able to find the trail head at the south end of the rock clearing.

Finally, just before 9 O'Clock, and long after the last of the other groups had left, our guide showed up. He was in full scout uniform, with very neat hiking boots and all. Very good looking compared to our hillbilly group with tee shirts, blue jeans, old tennis shoes or combat boots. We all assembled around the guide and Mr. Owens, our leader, for our instructions.

"OK, listen up. My name is Lester (I can't remember his real name). I am an Eagle Scout from Webster Groves. That's a suburb of St. Louis in case you don't know. I am very familiar with this trail, and my job is to make sure you don't get lost. I will be in the lead at all times. Nobody is to take even a step in front of me. If I go too fast for you, you will have to let me know and I will slow down for you. Again, under no circumstances are you to walk in front of me. Are there any questions?"

"No, let's get started!"

"Alright then – remember, stay behind me."

Eagle shit, for that's what we had resolved to call him, led the way out of the clearing and into the woods.

Glenn started grinning. "Hey, DeWayne, this is not the way to the trailhead."

"Maybe there is more than one place to start the trail."

"Nah, I don't think he knows where it is."

After traveling about a hundred yards into the woods – all of us trailing behind our guide – he called a halt.

"This is not the trail. Nobody move." ES walked to the back of our line and we did an about face to walk back the way we came.

The silence of the woods, formerly broken just by the chatter of alarmed squirrels and barks of Bluejays, was now smothered with cat-calls, whoops and laughter that brought a bright crimson to the cheeks of our guide. Another fifteen minutes were required for us to finally start at the trailhead that we had discovered earlier. Why didn't we tell ES where it was, if we were so anxious to get going and break the record? Are you kidding? And let him avoid all that embarrassment? No sir. He had started out with two strikes against him and then had completely struck out by being over an hour late, and then insulting our (self-proclaimed) intelligence by warning us not to step in front of him. No sir. He was going to regret he had ever heard of our group or the Taum Sauk Trail.

"Hey, let's pace this guy."

"What do you mean?"

"One of us will walk with ES and make polite conversation, but walking just a fraction faster than him. He won't be able to tolerate that, and will pick up the pace. The rest of us will lay back at a leisurely pace for half an hour or so, and then one of us will come up and take the pace while the first pacer hangs back to relax. We'll have him worn out in a couple of hours."

"That's brilliant! Let's do it."

Glenn took the first lead, while the rest of us hung back.

"Hey, Lester, how are you? My name is Glenn."

"I'm fine, Glenn. Hey, don't get in front of me."

"Oh, sorry. Guess I am just anxious to finish this trail today. It sure is hot, though."

Lester had held out his arms like a toll gate to keep Glenn from getting in front of him. Glenn kept up the small talk for half an hour, all the time pressing ES to walk faster without saying anything about it. The rest of us hung back, snickering into our armpits so Lester wouldn't become suspicious.

After a while I moved up and Glenn dropped back.

"Hi, Lester. I'm DeWayne. Where did you say you were from?" Lester held his arms out like an old mother hen, keeping me behind him.

And so it went for a couple of hours. Finally, we got the idea that one of us could engage ES on one side while another could walk past him on the other. That was even better. Lester had to jog a couple of steps to catch up with the offending wayward scout, causing him to break stride and interrupt his breathing rhythm. Then there were two scouts breaking ranks, then three, and finally around noon, ES gave up and just yelled at all of us as we jogged past him.

Now we were really making some time. Even though the temperature was approaching 95 degrees, we decided to see if we could jog all the way to the end. Soon we had caught up with the last group to leave the trailhead that morning. They were sitting on rocks and logs at the side of the trail, uniforms soaked through, and looking like last week's roses. They all looked up with undisguised disbelief at this troop of loonies jogging in the heat. We could hear them all talking excitedly among themselves as we passed by, and we loved it. We were even more determined to jog all the way to the end.

Mr. Owens had already dashed our hopes of attempting a new record by telling us that we were not going to hike the whole trail that day. Arrangements had already been made to have all our gear brought to a campground at about the halfway point. We argued vehemently, but to no avail. The truck would be driven to the campground, and that was that.

Since we couldn't attempt a new record for the whole trail we resolved to be the first group into camp that evening, even though the first group to begin that morning had had more than a two-hour head start on us. As we continued to jog along, Glenn and I eventually outdistanced everyone else and we saw a sign leading us to the summit of Taum Sauk Mountain. We followed it up to the peak, which was really a relatively flat, high plateau. There were mountains of large stone stacked several stories high, ringing the entire plateau. We had no idea what it was, but there was undoubtedly a large construction project in the works. After we had seen enough of that we started back down and began hearing voices shouting our names, so we hurried back to the trail. Mr. Owens had rightly guessed that we could not pass up the opportunity to explore on our own, so had held up the rest of the group at the fork and began calling for us.

What we didn't know then was that the electric power utility company in that area had been having some capacity issues and had received permission to alleviate that problem by building two artificial lakes; one at the top of Taum Sauk Mountain, and another at the base. The idea was to pump water to the top during nighttime hours, and then reverse the process during the peak-demand daytime hours, and run the water through turbines as it raced into the lower lake.

We were not very popular at that point, for causing some anxiety among the leaders and other boys. However, we resumed the trail and took up our jogging again. We had not seen ES since about noon and had no idea how far behind us he was.

We continued to pass other groups all day and eventually achieved our goal of being the first ones to the campsite, having passed all seven other groups. The truck was there with all our gear so we unloaded it and began setting up camp. Since we were the first ones there we had first choice for the best site. We had established our campsite and built our fire for dinner before any of the other groups appeared. We could hear conversations from the other groups all evening about 'those crazy idiots who ran the whole trail in this heat'. We were very proud.

Our 'guide' came dragging in long after we had eaten. I am not even sure he stayed overnight or accompanied us the next day for the remainder of the trail. Mr. Owens gave us a mild scolding for treating him the way we had, and we felt somewhat abashed at our behavior. Being the airheads we were however, we were not affected by it the next day at all.

Even though we continued to grouse about not being able to break the record for shortest time hiking the trail we were all very tired and fell exhausted into our tents after a short time of talking about the adventures of the day.

The following morning Mr. Owens drug out the largest skillet I have ever seen. We put five dozen eggs and a pound of butter into it, and had a wonderful breakfast of scrambled eggs and bacon. We broke camp, policed the area, and loaded our gear onto the truck that had brought us to the trailhead at Elephant Rocks. Someone then began the drive to Johnson's Shut-Ins, where they would meet us at the end of the day to take us back home.

ES was nowhere to be seen the next morning either, so we were free to finish the remainder of the hike by ourselves. After breaking camp, we headed back into the trail at a more leisurely pace this time, since we had no chance of trying for any kind of record and there was really no reason to rush. The rest of the hike was rather anticlimactic, not the least because ES was no longer there to torment. However, it was also very hot and we had really tired ourselves out the day before. Most of us had already gone through our extra socks, so several of us developed some bothersome blisters. That didn't dampen our spirits however, because we were all anticipating a really cool swimming session at the Shut-Ins.

After several hours, we could hear the Shut-Ins before we saw them. As we strolled into the park the scene was like an oasis. The river flowed over a series of large boulders for about 100 yards, creating a lot of noise, and a mist that rose up to cool our very hot and tired faces. As the water cascaded down and between the boulders, it formed several raceways and created a natural set of water slides.

While all that water raced and sluiced between the rocks in its way, one could walk across the river in dry feet by hopping from stone to stone. We ran across the river to the area the truck was waiting for us and stripped off our shirts, boots and socks. Then we made a beeline for the water.

All one had to do was wade into the river, sit down between a couple of boulders and let go. The current then shot us downstream, sliding along the slick rock and dropped us into a short waterfall. The backwash under the fall sucked me back under the overhang momentarily, but then spit me out downstream a few feet. It was glorious!

About an hour of that completely wore all of us out. Our leaders didn't have to work too hard to persuade us it was time to go back home, so we gathered all our clothes and climbed into the back of the stake truck for the ride home.

We were all talking about the great time we had for the last two days and recounting all the adventures with ES and passing all the other hiking groups, but it wasn't long before we were all sound asleep. The air whistling through the stake truck was cool and comforting and the excitement coupled with the effort of the hike and camping experience had drained us of all energy.

As for myself, I was dreading the return home. I never knew what to expect at these times, but I always knew it would not be pleasant. My thoughts turned to a church camping trip at Cresswell Park. Our Royal Ambassador counselor had dropped us off at the church (which was just down and across the street from our house) Saturday afternoon, and I had returned home with my duffel bag over my shoulder. I entered our living room, dropped my bag inside the door and walked across the room to the windows that looked back toward the church. I stood there for a few seconds thinking about the weekend we had just had and enjoying the memories of the campout, fishing and good times with my RA friends.

All of a sudden, I felt the sting of my mother's ever-present belt whaling across my back, buttocks and legs. She was screaming something but

I couldn't make it out, what with my yelling and the sound of the belt thrashing my body and whipping around the furniture. That went on for what seemed like several minutes, although I am sure it was only a few seconds, then her anger was spent. I never did know what set her off or what I had done, if anything, to ignite her outburst. I just knew that after several lashes her energy was spent, and she just walked away telling me I needed to clean up, or something. As usual, I just took the lashing and tried to get out of her presence as quickly as I could.

Mommy Dearest

My mother was a beautiful woman when she was young, the daughter of a poor Irish farmer. She married quite young and had eight pregnancies, six of which were successful. The first two ended in a miscarriage and a still birth. She was always very protective of us, and very careful about where she let us go. As I grew up and became aware of those first two lost siblings, I assumed that her first two unsuccessful births were the main reason for that. One of my oldest cousins told me that at one time she had been of a somewhat even temperament, but that at some point in her adult life she seems to have suffered some emotional event that changed her life, and consequently all our lives. Whatever it was must have happened early, because I cannot recall a time when she was not prone to violent outbursts of temper which most always resulted in long, shrill and very loud strings of screaming, and usually someone getting beaten with a switch, belt, or whatever else was handy.

During my adult life, I have had time to reflect that perhaps there is something to the supposed tendency of the Irish to be plagued with fits of depression. Also, Mother wanted to be a nurse, and Dad had always refused, saying that he didn't want her touching other men, or words to that effect. I know that the loss of her first two children affected her deeply, and she also had to deal with the facts that her father-in-law didn't like her, and that Dad's business had fallen on hard times after WWII, ending in bankruptcy. Mother's life had been filled with disappointment, frustration and loss, which had to weigh heavily on her mind. I will never really know the reasons for her behavior, and it is too bad that she didn't have the benefit of some therapy. I could have skipped over all of this, but I didn't think this story would be complete without touching on events that affected all of us very deeply, even into our children's lives.

There was a silver maple behind the house that had pushed up numerous root sprouts around its trunk. Most of those were just right for switches. Whenever David or I had done something to displease Mom, she would send us out to that tree to cut a switch for her so she could whip us with it. The walk back to the house from that tree was only about a hundred feet, but it seemed like a mile. Of course, we would try to choose a small switch that would break easily, but she was wise to that. If it broke before she was satisfied with the thrashing, we had to get another one and start all over. There was no fixed number of lashes for any offense, it just lasted until her anger was sated.

Mealtimes were not a pleasant time for any of us, either. Our dining room had three windows and a window seat that ran under the length of the three. That was where the three youngest of us sat; Jane, David and me. Dad sat on one end and Jerry, the oldest brother, sat at the other end. Mom usually sat across from the window seat. Many times, if not most, Mom would sit at the table with a belt draped across her shoulder just in case one of us should misbehave. As often as not, one of us would get a thrashing right at the table. She would jump up from her chair, reach for the belt and come around to the window seat, where she would lay into the offending culprit. If the intended victim was in the middle or on the far end, it was up to the other two to duck under the table or lean away from the flailing belt, which usually struck more than one person with every lash. The offense might have been something as terrible as one of us saying we didn't like the butter beans, or whatever. Or, it may have been an argument between two of us that precipitated the onslaught. We didn't always know what had caused it. I remember very little conversation at the table of any kind. I know I couldn't wait to finish dinner and get out of there. David had a different problem. He was a slow eater, and several times the rest of us would have finished, left the table, and most of the dishes were washed while he sat there by himself. We were not allowed to leave the table with food on our plate. If we took it, we ate it.

In my bedroom one time, she came at me with a handful of pants stretchers (expandable aluminum frames that one would insert down the legs of just-washed blue jeans for drying, so they wouldn't wrinkle or shrink) and began beating me over the head and shoulders with them, accompanied by the usual screaming that I couldn't understand. I was cowering, with my hands over my head trying to ward off the blows from the stretchers. I was probably screaming as well but had no idea what had set her off. Dad came when he heard the commotion and had to pull her off me. He called her name a couple of times trying to get her attention, and finally grabbed her hands to stop the beating, and said, "That's enough." She seemed to wilt as if she couldn't remember why she was beating me in the first place, and they both walked out of the room and left me there.

I am sure I had done something to upset her but for the life of me, I cannot remember what it might have been, nor do I remember knowing it at the time. Being a middle child anyway, and due to the constant tension in the house, I made every attempt to retreat from it whenever I had the chance, and to make myself invisible. I couldn't wait to be old enough to get a job; not only to have my own money, but so that I would have someplace to go.

We didn't take many vacations because of the need to take care of all the animals and gather eggs every day. Mom had always wanted to see the Grand Canyon though, and when I was twelve, with the hatchery and feed business about gone, we took Jerry's 1956 Buick on a week long trip to see it. Jerry and Maxine didn't go because they were working, so it was just Mom, Dad, Janet, David, Jane and me. I said 'just', but that's six people in a car for a week-long, 2,500-mile car trip. It can get very crowded.

Dad knew we could just about take Route 66 all the way there, so we went southwest through Joplin, Missouri, into Oklahoma and then into the Texas panhandle. I never saw so many oil wells in my life! They were in people's yards, along the highway, in the middle of a drive-in theatre – everywhere.

We were driving through Texas that first evening and were hit with the worst thunderstorm I have ever witnessed. Rain came down in buckets and Dad had to pull over to wait until visibility improved. We sat there for perhaps half an hour, during which time Mom decided she didn't really want to see the Grand Canyon after all, but maybe go see someone they knew in Colorado Springs! We got a room in a small motel for the night, and in the morning headed northwest to Colorado.

When we got to Colorado, whomever we came to see wasn't home, so we motored through the Garden of the Gods and Cripple Creek. Then it was time to start home. Colorado was beautiful, and driving back east through Kansas was interesting for a while. We didn't normally stop at restaurants to eat; Mom packed bread and bologna and we made sandwiches at roadside rest stops. To slake our thirst, we bought bags of ice and carried it in a Scotty cooler. We munched ice during the day and during our meal stops.

We could see the aftermath of dust storms all along the highway. In places we could only see the tops of fenceposts; most of them buried in dry dust and sand. Somewhere in the middle of Kansas the water pump went out on the Buick and we had to stop for repairs. The Buick dealer where we stopped didn't have a water pump, and we had to wait for one to be delivered from another town that afternoon. Mom spread out our blanket on the ground in a park by the garage, and we settled down and ate lunch while we waited. I was lying on my back after lunch when Mom walked by the blanket and decided I was trying to look up her dress, and began whaling on me with her belt. We finally made it home, and I was just as happy to be able to separate myself from her and put some distance between us again.

Temper, Temper...

Our class was not immune to the moods and actions typical of many adolescents, and as we entered sixth grade, that was very much in evidence. We had a teacher we referred to as Wild Bill, who was very proud of the paddle that he carried with him at all times. Wild Bill made frequent use of that paddle, and in fact began to break several of them. Pretty soon, he was carrying two of them at a time; one in each inside pocket of his sport jacket.

The first time I was called to the front to receive one of Wild Bill's blessings, I remember being somewhat afraid that I would embarrass myself in front of the class. He told me to bend over the desk, and then he applied one of his enforcers rather diligently several times to my backside. After a few whacks, I began to relax – I had had worse at home. I could tolerate this.

After a while, there arose a sort of competition among a few of us – all boys, of course. We began to keep score. Our goal was to win the race for the most whuppins during the semester. I believe Chuck won that race, with about 56. I came in a poor second, with somewhere in the low 30's.

There was a student who seemed to be a trouble magnet – it just followed him around. We were playing dodgeball in the gym one day, and he did something to rile the gym teacher – I don't know what it was. The teacher strode purposefully to the center of the floor, and grabbed him around the neck. I don't know what he said, but it was not exactly to the teacher's liking. He picked him up by the seat of his gym shorts and the back of his T shirt, and threw him half way across the floor, into the bleachers on the side. I thought sure he was killed, but he just got up and sat down on the bench. That pretty much took the steam out of the room, and the rest of the period was pretty quiet.

That happened in the fall, when the weather was cool and damp, so that we had to have our gym class indoors. In the spring it was time for softball, and our gym teacher organized a game by dividing the class into two teams. There were really too many kids for just nine players on each team so the extra kids just filled in the extra spaces between first and second base, left and center field, etc. The same boy was positioned as sort of a short second baseman, behind the pitcher, but in front of the second baseman. I think he got bored with the lack of activity and began picking up pebbles and tossing them at the back of the pitcher. I am sure there was no sinister or malicious motive behind that, it was just the thoughtless actions of a bored kid. However, it caught the attention of the teacher, and the scenario from the previous fall was played out on the ball diamond. Teacher caught him from behind, grabbed him by the neck and the seat of his shorts, and threw him into the bench that served as a dugout, by the first base line. The throw landed him just short of the bench, where he landed on all fours, and slid into the bench, raising dust along the way. He just got up and sat down on the bench, in his morose way, with his elbows on his knees, and his head in his hands. There was no joy in Mudville after that.

The Dark Side

Most people that I knew were decent people, and I actually felt safer away from home than in it. I almost always had the impression that everyone had my best interests at heart. However, there were exceptions that I discovered the hard way.

We were visiting one of my favorite cousins one Sunday, and I persuaded Donnie to let me ride his bicycle around the block. They lived on a bluff in Washington, in view of the Missouri River as it wound its way through the city. My plan was to just ride around the block – how hard could that be? Just ride down the street, turn left at every corner, and I would come right back to his house, right? Well, the streets weren't all at right angles and pretty soon I was hopelessly lost. I tried to turn around and retrace my progress, but that didn't work either.

I noticed a young man on the sidewalk and stopped to ask him for directions. He said sure, he could show me the way back. Just follow him to the back yard and we could see the street I needed across the alley. He seemed very friendly and kept pointing across the back yard as we walked. "See, your street is right over there. Can't see it yet? Let's walk a little further."

There was a small tool shed at the back of the property, and as we reached it he opened the door and pulled me in. When he unzipped his jeans and began to pull his pants down I began to sniffle because I was really scared. Then as he began to pull my jeans off me, I began to cry. He tried to assault me but I was not cooperating, because I was crying and obviously in great distress. After he stroked me several times and was not getting anywhere with me he finally gave up. He told me to pull my pants back up, pulled me out of the shed and showed me the way back home. I pedaled that bike for all it was worth and dried my eyes as best I could before I got back. I was so ashamed I never mentioned it to anyone.

My small circle of friends was my greatest support. We talked about many things, including how to handle certain unpleasant situations. When we were Freshmen we were talking one day, and one of them (I am not going to mention names) said, "You need to be careful around Mr. _____".

"Why is that? He seems like a really nice teacher to me. I think he is one of my favorites."

"He was my favorite teacher too. But, he invited me to his house last week to 'help me with some lessons'. While I was there we worked on the lessons for a while, then he got out some kind of lotion and some towels, and suggested that we rub the lotion on each other."

"What did you do?"

"I told him I didn't think that would be a good idea, picked up my stuff and left."

Here was a perfect opportunity for me to share my experience from a few years before, but I couldn't do it. I was still too ashamed. But, we all agreed that we would watch out for Mr._____, and report to each other in case of another incident. We also agreed to keep a wary eye out for any other teacher that might seem to be doing the same thing. Curiously, none of us thought of contacting school administration, or our parents either. Perhaps that's why so many people get away with it. The shame and embarrassment results in silence.

Frank and his sister were very quiet kids, liked by everyone although not seemingly close to anyone. Frank and I had a good, friendly relationship. We spoke often, before or after class, but never during class. Frank and his sister were both too polite to misbehave in class, or anywhere for that matter. At some point, Frank and I began to discuss coins because I was collecting Indian head pennies, buffalo nickels, Liberty dollars, etc. Frank gave me a handful of foreign coins from all over the world. Later, he came to me with a small cloth bag full of coins and just gave them to me. I think he was also giving other things to other kids, but I am not sure about that. I wish that I had known what it means when a child begins to give away cherished items. I would like to think that I would have alerted somebody. Frank later committed suicide, and as an adult I look back and can see the indications of severe depression. I am very saddened by the loss of such a gentle person, not only to me but to the world in general.

As I became a teenager, I was hit with the curse of my Irish ancestry on my mother's side – depression. Normally, I was a gregarious sort of guy with an active, if somewhat twisted sense of humor. I loved to tell jokes, be the center of attention, and interact with others around me. At unexpected times though, it would hit me like a hammer. All of a sudden, I would feel a strong urge to be by myself and withdraw from all conversation with anyone. This often happened when I was in the middle of a group of friends. I would just walk away and stare off into the distance. I could be with my girlfriend Gail, and I would not say a word for a whole afternoon or evening. I don't know why she stayed with me. It must have been love (doesn't speak well for her sense of judgement).

Get a Job

In 1957, The Silhouettes released a song titled "Get A Job" that rose to number one on the billboard charts. The song really captured the mood, especially of young people at the time as the country was entering a recession, and everyone was looking for a job. Several of my friends' fathers worked at one of the auto plants in St. Louis, and most of them had been laid off by the middle of 1958. The street that ran in front of our house, Springfield Avenue, was repaved that summer and I can recall seeing some of those parents working on the paving gang as day laborers in an effort to make ends meet.

So many adults out of work and taking minimum-wage jobs just to get by made it even more difficult for young people to find work. Of course, at that time I was only twelve but my friends and I talked a lot about finding work somewhere to earn spending money. None of us received allowances or money from our parents for doing chores around the house. It just wasn't done at that time and besides, our parents had precious little money anyway. I did as much as I could to help in the feed store by waiting on customers and unloading trucks as they came in, but I also continued to look for opportunities to make "real money".

Mom helped me respond to an ad in the Sunday magazine that said I could make a lot of money selling Christmas cards. I sent in my few dollars and received a catalog and a beginning inventory of sample cards. I put all that into our rather large picnic basket and began walking around town, pestering our friends and neighbors to buy their Christmas cards from me. I did well enough the first year that I had enough to buy a few presents for my parents. The second year I did even better, and had enough left after Christmas to buy a few trinkets for myself. I'm sure everyone in town was relieved when I became old enough to get a real job and stop bothering them with my Fuller Brush act.

The Newspaper

St. Clair had a weekly newspaper called The St. Clair Chronicle. Dorothy, the owner, publisher, editor, reporter and photographer of the paper knew our family, and Jerry had had a job there as a linotype operator. She had really liked his work. He had since left the paper and launched his own effort at raising chickens and selling eggs to local stores. As soon as I was 15 I applied for a Social Security card, and went to see Dorothy about working there. She was nice enough to give me a start as a printer's devil, at the respectable sum of $0.65/hour.

My initial duties were to sweep, dust and generally clean up around the print shop. After a month or so, I was also given the responsibility of making sure there was enough lead available in the form of "pigs" for the linotype machine. I was also given a raise to the great wage of $0.75/hour!!

The linotype operator would type the copy for the newspaper from typed or written manuscripts from Dorothy or other reporters. Lead was fed into a hopper at the back of the machine, that was heated to keep the lead molten. As the operator typed in the copy, the machine would create strips of type that were one column wide, one line high, and about one-inch deep, with the letters and words essentially melted into the thin face. These strips would then be arranged into a clamp that constituted a page, and loaded into the printing press.

After the paper was printed all those strips were essentially useless, and were re-melted to be used in the next issue. I collected those and took them to a small gas-fired furnace at the back of the shop. After pouring the bars into the furnace and lighting the burners, flux was added to draw the dross to the top. That was then skimmed off and disposed of and the molten lead was then ladled into small bars, or pigs, that looked like small silver bars.

Of course, the lead didn't immediately melt. It took some time for that to happen, so after getting the furnace going, I would do whatever else needed to be done. The problem was that, at some point the burners needed to be turned down to avoid vaporizing the lead. I could never remember to come back and recheck the furnace, so the back of the shop would fill up with smoke, and someone from the printing crew would have to yell for me to come and turn it down. I'm afraid my attention deficit disorder was very evident at that stage. Although it didn't get me fired, it caused some great upset every time I smoked the office and shop.

Some parts of the newspaper, mostly the advertisements, were not done using the linotype. Those were done with hand-set type, using individual letters. At my request, I was given the opportunity to try my hand at hand-setting type, and I think I did pretty well at it. The difficult part was that the letters are backwards and have to be loaded upside down. I was told that this is where the phrase, "mind your Ps and Qs" came from, since the lower-case p looks like a q when you're loading it backwards.

"DeWayne, Mr. Clark wants to see you in his office right away."

My high school home room teacher had just delivered an ominous message to me. Why would the principal want to see me? God knows I had been called into the office enough times before, but I could think of no good reason for him to call me now. I had dressed appropriately for once; I had not left another snake in a teacher's desk drawer; I hadn't recently played any pranks on anyone. What could it be? I trudged down the hall, turned right, and ambled down another long hall toward the front of the school where the glass-walled principal's office was.

As I walked into the office, Mr. Clark's secretary gave me the look that said, 'I am so ashamed of your behavior.' "Mr. Clark is expecting you. Go right in."

I hesitated at the open doorway. "Mr. Clark, you wanted to see me?"

Mr. Clark looked up without rising from his chair behind the massive principal's desk. "Come in, DeWayne. Please sit down."

I sat in one of the two visitor's chairs across the desk from Mr. Clark. Then I saw it. He had my wallet on the desk in front of him. My spirits brightened immediately, because I had lost the wallet sometime during or after the recent basketball game at school. My tension-filled face quickly changed to an ear-to-ear smile. "Oh great, I see someone found my wallet."

"Yes, the janitor found it after the game under the bleachers."

"It must have fallen out of my back pocket. I couldn't imagine what had happened to it." I reached for the wallet, but Mr. Clark pulled it back. He reached into it and pulled out four lunch tickets, of different colors.

"I need to talk to you about these, DeWayne. What are you doing with unissued lunch tickets, and where did you get them?"

My smile vanished in a nanosecond (was there such a thing as a nano back then?). I was really in trouble. I knew that I had to do some fast explaining and it had better be good. Fortunately, I figured the truth was my best hope for salvation.

"I work at the Chronicle after school, and one of my jobs is to print and cut the lunch tickets. Sometimes a few of the tickets are smudged, or we have an overrun, and those tickets are destroyed. I thought it would be fun to be able to tease my friends by having a ticket of each color that I would pretend to use for lunch. I never actually used any of them and it was just for a prank. You can check the records and see that I have bought a lunch ticket every week."

"We already have checked and that's true, we show that you have purchased a lunch ticket every week. We couldn't figure out, though, why anyone in their right mind would expose themselves to potential trouble by even having these obviously fraudulent tickets. Have you been giving any of them away?"

"No, I wouldn't do that; that would be stealing!"

"But, you stole the tickets in the first place."

"I guess I didn't see it as stealing, since they were over-runs and were going to be destroyed anyway."

He reached across the desk and handed my wallet back to me, sans tickets. "Whether you stole or not, doing what you did could have given other people the idea that you did, and perhaps given them the idea that they could try that too. It wasn't very smart on your part, don't you think?"

"Yes sir. I won't do it again."

"See that you don't. Now I suggest you get back to class."

"Thank you, Mr. Clark."

He nodded, and I rose from my chair. I had a powerful urge to get to the bathroom and check my underwear. On the way back to class, I had the thought that he might call Dorothy and tell her I had absconded with some of her merchandise. If he did that, I would lose my job. I couldn't concentrate the rest of the day. All I could think about was what would happen when I walked into the Chronicle that afternoon. Would I be drawn and quartered, fired, forgiven? Even worse, what would Mr. Clark and others who knew about this think of me? Others' impressions of me were (and still are) very important to me, and I couldn't stand the thought of being considered a thief.

Mr. Clark either didn't call my employer or she decided it was not worth mentioning, because nothing happened. When I got to work that afternoon, nothing was said. I was thankful to Mr. Clark for being so understanding and decided to try to straighten up. That thought stuck with me for at least the rest of the afternoon. Unfortunately, I was soon back to my normal self.

With my religious upbringing, I was somewhat familiar with the Bible, and my favorite apostle and author was St. Paul. One of his statements that always stuck with me, and does to this day, was his lament that…'those things that I should do, I do not, and those things that I should not do, I do…' Actually, that gave me hope, since, if such an obviously good man could stray from time to time, maybe there was hope for me.

ROUTE 66

Route 66 was officially designated in 1926, as a route connecting Chicago and Los Angeles, and following a route that connected rural and urban towns and cities along the way. It was worked on heavily during the depression, thus furnishing jobs to thousands of unemployed youths during those desperate years. By 1938 it was declared completely paved. At St. Clair, it had been a single 2-lane ribbon of concrete that ran generally southwest to northeast through central Missouri. At some point, the road was improved to provide two lanes in each direction with a median so wide that at times you could not even see the opposite lanes. Then, the Eisenhower Interstate System began to expand in earnest in the mid-50's. St. Clair had sort of grown around the highway as it cut through the area southwest of St. Louis.

As the new four-lane highway was laid out, the engineers naturally took the opportunity to improve the route either by straightening the highway, or improving the grade by cutting through hills and filling in valleys. Primarily, this was because the law that created the Interstate System was created for defense purposes, as the Cold War ramped up. One of the requirements written into that law was that at least one mile in every five miles of road in the system had to be straight and relatively level, so military aircraft could land and take off using the highway. In some areas, the old roadbed was used for either the east- or westbound sides, and in other places the new route deviated completely from the old route so that the old highway now laid either north or south of the new route.

As the new highway came abreast of St. Clair, it moved about one-half mile to the north, leaving the little town behind. However, the construction provided many jobs for local out-of-work people for several years. As the highway moved west it swung back to the south of the old route.

Since the new 66 was not a limited access highway yet, people didn't have to drive for miles between exits; side roads continued to intersect the new highway at frequent intervals, and without entrance and exit ramps. Businesses that had been located on the old route and were lucky enough to be close to the new route, continued to flourish. Filling stations and motor hotels, or motels, were sprinkled on both sides of the highway along its entire route, from Chicago to the Pacific Ocean at southern California. One of those businesses close to St. Clair was a gas station, serviced by one of our renters, named Sherman. He had the franchise for St. Clair and the surrounding community.

During the winter of 1961, Sherman contracted the mumps. Since he was an adult, it really hit him hard, and put him down to bedrest for more than two weeks. At the same time, we were hit with a near-record cold wave. Temperatures plummeted to 27 degrees below zero, and stayed very cold for several days! Everybody was calling for heating oil, and he could not deliver. Although Pete, Janice's father, was working for him at the time he could not keep up working alone. In addition to just the volume of business, the heating oil became so cold in the storage tanks that it would barely flow. Just refilling the delivery truck took a lot longer than usual.

The situation became critical because, as usual, some customers waited until their own supply was dangerously low before ordering a refill, and with the higher usage rate brought on by the record cold some of them were running out. Sherman asked my parents if I could help out, and of course I was only too happy to be given the opportunity to earn a little extra money.

The problem was that I had no real cold weather gear. I had a winter jacket of course, for walking to school, but that did not provide any long-term protection against this kind of weather. I also had no winter gloves, socks or boots. I borrowed Jerry's winter army coat, which was better than nothing, but not really well insulated. Then I went downtown and bought a pair of wool boot socks and some boots, which would keep out the moisture from snow and ice, but weren't insulated. I donned a pair of work gloves, and with that I jumped into the truck with Pete and spent the rest of the week trying to stay warm and avoid frostbite as we filled as many heating oil tanks as we could.

By the end of the week, I had come to appreciate people who have to work outside all year. I had managed to avoid frostbite, but I was miserable the whole time. The little money I had earned was well-earned, and I was very tired. We had worked pretty much from sunup to after dark every day for a week, and helped to relight numerous pilot lights for people.

That wasn't the only issue with the cold temperature however. Jerry was deep into the poultry business at that time, and had a few thousand egg layers that produced eggs which Jerry used to supply several grocery stores in the area. A couple thousand of those chickens were housed on Dad's property in one of his coops, but a few thousand were also housed at a remote site about two miles out of town. There was no real provision to supply heat to either of those locations, and although they huddled together as best they could, dozens of them died every night for awhile during the cold snap. Many of them froze; I suspect some of them were just smothered at the bottom of the heaps of chickens trying to stay warm.

Another issue with the cold was water. Jerry put heat lamps and heat tapes in and around the water containers, and that helped. But there was no water source at the remote location, and we had to haul it in a thousand-gallon tank that we would load into Dad's truck. It took a good part of a day just to fill the tank. In fact, we couldn't fill the tank, because that would have overloaded the truck. We filled it about two-thirds full, which created another problem. There were no baffles in the tank, so when we started up, the water would rush to the back of the tank, creating a big reverse force on the truck so that the engine would really strain and threaten to stall. Then the water would change course, running to the front of the truck, causing the engine to speed up. It was a real trick with a manual transmission, trying to keep the engine from neither stalling or over-revving. Then we got to a stop sign, the same issues emerged in reverse. Water rushing forward wanted to overcome the brakes as we tried to stop the truck.

When we reached the remote property, we found that our problems had only begun. It had taken most of the day to fill the tank, and by the time we got to the hen house it was dark. Of course, the temperature had plunged, and it was very cold. Jerry had a very small rotary pump that was used to pump the water out of our tank into a holding tank in the building. Remember, I said it was dark? There was no light in the building, and we had to find the pump in the dark, and get it fastened to the tank on the truck as well as to the fitting on the holding tank. After several minutes we accomplished that task, and were looking forward to being able to sit in the truck with the heater going, to warm our frozen hands and feet.

Such was not to be however, because the valve at the holding tank had been frozen shut, and the blockage caused the pump to overwork and blew a fuse. Fumbling around in the dark, we finally located a box of fuses and replaced the blown one, all the while hoping we could keep our frozen fingers out of the wiring in the fuse box. We tried again, with the same result. How to thaw out the valve? Neither of us smoked, and didn't have any matches or lighter. We finally found some scraps of paper and used the cigarette lighter in the truck to heat the paper, which we then blew on to get it to ignite.

After holding the burning paper to the valve for a few seconds we tried again. This time the pump ran for a couple of seconds, until it froze, which blew another fuse. We went through a few more iterations of holding burning paper to various parts of the pump, valves and piping until we finally got it running. Then we sat in the truck for a long time while the pump did its thing. I don't think I have ever been so cold, before or since. Of course, our problems were repeated again and again for most every farmer in the area, as a lot of livestock died in the cold snap.

Girls and Cooties

As our class entered the seventh grade, we became the first class to attend the newly-constructed junior high facility that had been built onto the high school building about a mile from our house, on Highway 30. That meant that I had a much longer walk to school every day, instead of the short jaunt just across the street.

As I reached puberty, I began to think of girls as more than just friends. Rather than just going camping, hiking or fishing with the other guys, it somehow seemed to be much more important to spend some time with girls. However, there were dangers involved. It seems that somehow, girls had acquired a mysterious malady called COOTIES! What these were was entirely unknown, but were purportedly dangerous to boys, so one had to be careful. I don't know where this new-found knowledge originated but it must have been true, because every boy seemed to know about it. All of a sudden, every girl that we had known since first grade or before, was suddenly a source of contamination. I wondered if this sudden affliction had anything to do with the acquisition of breasts, since those two situations seemed to be occurring at the same time. So, walking down the school hallway, conversations would be like,

"Wow, would you look at her? She is really cute."

"Yeah, but be careful. She has cooties."

"What? Cooties?! How did that happen?"

"Well, you know she is really loose."

"Loose? How do you know that?"

"Well, she is dating a Junior. She must be."

So, that was the other thing. Some girls were labeled as 'loose'. That could be either exciting, or frightening, depending on your personality.

Somehow though, those afflictions seemed to vanish as we moved through Junior High and into High School; girls were suddenly cured of that terrible affliction. At any rate, there seemed to be something magic about spending time with a girl.

DeWayne and Janice, all dressed up

I mean, it was fun to go on a hayride with a girl you had asked and be able to put your arm around her waist, smell her soap and her hair, and show off how funny you could be. What was it about that? A funny feeling; a sort of peace and excitement at the same time.

I began to enjoy just walking downtown with someone, stopping in to Sincox', or Wards Rexall Drug Store for an ice cream soda, going to the show, or bowling. That was about it for entertainment in St. Clair. Our bowling alley was in the basement of one of the buildings on Main Street and had four alleys, with manual pin setters. Vernon was one of the pin setters. I could see him behind the pins, sitting on a stool back there. He would jump down after the ball was thrown, pick up the ball and put it in the gravity ball return, clear away the pins still on the alley, put them in the rack ready to be set again, and jump back onto the stool. Occasionally, when I had thrown a really bad shot he would throw an extra pin into the ones standing, and knock some more down for me. I could bowl half the day for fifty cents.

Our theatre was a small, filthy affair; you wanted to go to the bathroom before going to the show, because you sure didn't want to use the facility there. It usually showed horse operas, with a cartoon and maybe a newsreel with Lowell Thomas narrating.

Of course, all that cost money which I didn't have. Also, since I wasn't driving yet, I couldn't pick up a girl at her house. What to do? My solution was to ask a girl if she would meet me there – inside the lobby. That way, she had to get there herself and buy how own ticket. I soon realized that most of the girls were already dating guys who had their drivers' licenses, and many had their own cars. That cut the field down considerably. However, my scheme did work a few times, and for a while.

So, Gigi (not her real name) met me inside the lobby, I bought us some popcorn and sodas, and we made a beeline for the back row. We sat through the first feature and ate our popcorn, then I decided it was time for me to see if I could put my arm around her. I slid my arm up to her shoulder and rested my hand on her neck. *'maybe if I take it slow, I can get all the way to her other shoulder'.* Thirty minutes later, my hand had slithered almost to her other shoulder. *'I'm really moving now!'*

At that point, she lost patience with me, grabbed my hand and clamped it down on her not insubstantial left breast. *'So, that's what they feel like'*. I was so shy, I couldn't speak. I just sat there for the rest of the movie like that – didn't even try to kiss her! I was such a Casanova.

I think she decided I wasn't the person for her; we didn't go out again together. There were other opportunities however. Several times, I was asked to go with a girl and her parents to church functions like spaghetti suppers or other events, but of course that was not too exciting. I had to get a job so I could start saving for date money.

My friend, Gary, and I used to meet up about half way to school and finish our walk together. Both of us lived too close to school to be able to ride the bus, even though we had to cross a state highway to get there. The walk was actually fun with a friend to talk to, except in the winter when the weather got cold, and especially if there was some snow.

Our music teacher drove the same route to get to school, and we flagged her down one time for a ride. After that, if we saw her, we would try to flag her down, but usually she would ignore us. We had no idea about liability.

One particularly snowy day, we saw her car approaching, and we both grabbed door handles and held on as she dragged us down the street, our feet sliding in the slush. She finally relented and let us in, thinking she was going to drag us under her car. We got a little lecture about the wisdom of taking that chance. After that, we understood we had overplayed our hands, and just walked.

Athletics

I had tried to play baseball when the Khoury League came to town, but my vision did not allow me to be a very good player. I did play first base, but was a terrible hitter. I just could not see the ball. The last straw for that effort was a hot summer when I was about thirteen.

Mrs. Crecelius had a strawberry patch about a mile west of our house on Springfield Road, across Highway 30. The Crecelius family had lived on a farm way out of town (I mean, remote!), but had recently moved to town, and she kept this strawberry patch on some ground that had belonged to the Frost family.

I had volunteered to help her weed the strawberries, and was stooped over pulling weeds. The next thing I remember is that I was sitting up, propped against the wall of a small tool shed on the north side, out of the sun. Mrs. Crecelius was still out there weeding the strawberries. I tried to get up but everything went black, I became very dizzy, and fell back down, so I just sat there for a while. She looked up and laughed, "back with us?" I don't think I answered because I couldn't quite figure out where I was, or why I was sitting against this shed. She finally finished weeding and came over to the shed to put away her hoe. As she opened the door next to me, there was a copperhead stretched across the threshold.

Mrs. Crecelius was a large woman, and at least sixty years old, but she jumped right over that snake, into the shed, and retrieved a hatchet. She cut the head off that snake without flinching. I would not have dared to get my hands close enough to do that, with that short-handled hatchet, but she did.

I don't remember how we got home. Maybe someone came to give us a ride back. At any rate, I could not do anything physical for the rest of the summer. I tried for a couple of baseball games to play my position at first base, but could not even perform the infield practice. Just throwing the ball a couple of times caused me to faint. I was worthless for the rest of the summer.

When I reached high school, I tried out for basketball but quickly realized that I did not have the eye—hand coordination to be any good. I suited up a few times with the B team, but never played much, so gave up on that sport.

Running, however, was something I could do, and enjoyed very much. I had raced against classmates during recess since grade school, and was faster than most of them. I signed up for Athletics class. To be considered for that class, which was more rigorous than "Gym", one had to participate in one of the competitive sports and I decided that Track was the place I would earn my spot in the class.

Coach Sullivan tried to get me interested in hurdles because of my long legs, but I had seen what happened to anyone who became tangled up in one of those and decided against it, after a few tries. We had a cinder track, and tumbling down into those sharp stones guaranteed a lot of painful scrapes and cuts.

I was not quite fast enough out of the blocks for the 100-yard dash, but I did compete in it. My best event was the 220-yard dash, where I had time to make up for my sloth out of the blocks. I also competed in the 440-yard dash, but really suffered through it due to my lack of stamina. The 880-yard dash and mile were beyond me. So, the 100 and 220 were my races, along with the 4 by 100 and 4 by 220 relays, and I typically ran in all four events at every track meet.

Coach Sullivan had an active and dry sense of humor. At one of our track meets, he gathered us around before the 440 event, and said, "ok, we're racing against a very good team today, so we need a racing strategy. The strategy for today is for all of you (I think there were three of us in this race) to start the race as fast as you can go, (and here he paused briefly) and then gradually pick up speed."

That got a good laugh, and broke the tension for us so we could concentrate on the race without being so nervous. I was feeling pretty good, because I had been awarded one of the new pairs of track spikes. Our school didn't have enough money to provide track spikes for every runner, so Coach parceled them out to those few who had the best chance of benefitting from them. The rest of us wore our own tennis shoes.

When the gun went off, I got a good start off the line and by the first turn I found myself in second place behind Denver, a country boy from Lonedell who attended our school. I was feeling very good about my position, comfortable with the thought that I would never beat Denver, so if I could stay right behind him, we would at least have first and second.

As I rounded the second turn and started down the back straightaway, I began to really stretch for more speed when my jock strap broke and snapped me (and Willy) to attention. I think I jumped about two feet straight up at the shock, but then tried to get back into my rhythm through the pain. I had lost a stride or two and needed to make up some time, but then noticed that Little Jimmy was peaking through the bottom of my shorts. I tried to push him back inside, but with every stride he came back out for another look. I continued limping along for the remaining 200 yards, trying to be unobtrusive about keeping my hand around my groin, and I think I came in fifth out of six runners.

At the next track meet, Coach made a point of calling all of us together and telling us to be sure and 'check all our equipment'. Very funny, coach.

Our school didn't have enough buses or budget to haul the track team to every meet, so quite often we students would pool up and drive in one of our cars. That was a lot of fun and we had some great adventures going to and coming from those events. As you could imagine, a car full of teenage boys was a great recipe for breaking speed limits, taking turns too fast, passing on double yellows, and all sorts of other mischief. Thinking back on it, we were very fortunate that there was not a major tragic accident during those trips.

When we went to major multi-school events, a bus was usually made available so the opportunity for vehicular mischief was minimized. However, we took the opportunity to make use of the extra storage capacity a long bus afforded. Since our school was so poor and had to make do with used and less than optimal equipment, we were always envious of the great equipment available to other teams.

The Conference track meet was held in Washington, where the best track was located. During my Junior year, we had a really good time. Leo was our shot putter; by far the biggest man on the team, and extremely strong. Gary was also a shot putter, a distant second to Leo. Three of us sauntered over to the pit, with a strategic plan in mind. As we walked up to the person officiating at the pit, I stepped forward and signed my name as the person representing St. Clair, along with Gary. I knew the rudiments of how to pitch the thing, but had never competed in the event.

I made my first pitch of three; form was okay, and I had tried my best, but it was a pretty pitiful effort. The competitor from Washington smirked and whispered something to one of his teammates, who threw his head back with a great roar of a laugh.

I said, "That's not too bad, but I think I can do better. Gary, see what you can do."

Gary stepped up, and lobbed the shot a respectable distance, several feet farther than my feeble effort.

"There, that's more like it", he said.

The guy from Washington stepped into the pit for his pitch, and threw a tremendous distance, well beyond both Gary's and my pitches.

"Now, that's the way it oughtta be done", he boasted, and swaggered back to his group.

Gary said (as had been pre-arranged), "Hey Leo, why don't you try this?"

"I don't know, how do ya throw that thang?"

"Just watch me next time, and do what I do."

So, he asked the scorer if he could sign up for the shot put, and the official said of course. Anyone from one of the teams could register.

My second throw wasn't any better than my first, but Gary's second throw went well beyond his first; still well short of the Washington pitch. The Washington competitor swaggered up to the line and fired off an impressive pitch that exceeded his first one by about a yard, then strutted back to his group with a smirk on his face aimed directly at us. The other teams competing in this event went through their pitches, but we were really concentrating on beating the Washington team, as the best equipped and trained of the bunch.

Finally, Leo stepped into the pit and said, "How do ya hold this thang agin?"

Gary showed him how to hold the ball in the crook of his neck, and how to turn and crouch at the back of the ring, so that he could spring forward and up while turning and extending his arm to release the shot.

Leo, as tutored, turned to the scorekeeper and said, "Can I have a practice throw?"

That produced a tremendous round of guffaws and howls from the other teams, with much backslapping. "No, the competition has started. You get three pitches, and we take the furthest one. Step in and take your first pitch."

So Leo stepped into the ring and, with a mighty grunt and show of force, threw the shot just short of the furthest pitch.

The other putters went through their last pitches, with the Washington competitor besting his second throw by a few inches. Then, Leo stepped up for his second pitch and launched a missile that went well beyond the last measurement arc. Frantic murmurs from the Washington crowd, and then immediate silence. Leo's last pitch was somewhat anticlimactic, but set a new meet record. We made a big show of congratulating Leo, slapping him on the back, and telling him he should consider signing up for this event at every meet. Competitors from the other teams congratulated Leo as well, except for the Washington team, who knew they had been had.

As usual, I raced in four events: 100, 220, and two relays. At some other events I had tried my luck on the 440-yard dash, but did not have the stamina for it. Denver however, seemed to be able to run forever. As the runners in his heat took off, Denver fell into line in second place, just behind the lead runner. As we watched the runners proceed around the track in a bunch, someone behind me said, "What happened to your great runner? I thought he was supposed to be so great."

I said, "keep your eyes on the halfway point, just across the track."

When the pack reached the halfway point, Denver leaned forward and looked as though he had suddenly shifted into overdrive. He passed the lead runner in about five steps and easily pulled away from the pack, leaving them far behind. At the finish line, Denver crossed alone, about four or five strides ahead of the next runner, with the rest of the pack farther back.

I didn't win my individual races, but I placed in both of them. I was happy with that though, as we swept first, second and third in both the 100 and 220-yard dashes. For some reason, I was also scheduled in the 4 x 440-yard relay. I ran second position, receiving a handoff from Larry, and then handing off to Glenn. Glenn had an interesting stride, with long, slow leaps that always reminded me of an Impala pronking. While his gait appeared to be slow, his strides were tremendously long, giving him impressive speed while appearing to be loafing.

As I rounded the fourth turn on my leg of the relay the Washington runner caught up and cut in front of me, raking my shin with his spikes. Switching lanes is permitted, as long as there is sufficient room so as not to impede or injure the other runner. In this case, the spiking of my leg caused me to stumble and nearly fall. However, I recovered and finished my leg, handing off to Glenn, even though I had lost about three steps.

The scuffle in my leg of the race produced a gap between us and the lead team that neither Glenn nor Denver, running anchor, were able to make up completely. As the race concluded, Denver was almost even with the Washington competitor but they held on to win. I was kicking myself for allowing our scuffle to cause me so many lost steps, when Larry dragged me to the race official, screaming about my injured leg due to the race interference. He looked down at my leg which was still bleeding profusely with blood running into my shoe, and declared us to be the winner of the race. The other coach knew he didn't have a leg to stand on (pardon the pun), and let the decision stand without counter protest.

We didn't realize it at the time, but with that win we had won every event in the meet. In some events we had taken all three places. The bus ride home was really noisy, as we congratulated each other on taking every trophy home for St. Clair.

When traveling to other major track meets, many times we had the use of one of the school buses. That was the case when we went to the Mineral Area Relays in southeast Missouri – I think it was in either Potosi or Sikeston. We considered this our most important event of the year. Although we went to the state track meet every year, we never felt we had any chance to win anything there. We felt more confident of being able to bring something home from the Mineral Area Relays.

It was intimidating to see all the athletes from Southeast Missouri, many in fine track shoes and uniforms, with fancy warmups and all kinds of other new equipment. We runners had our new track shoes but that was about it. Most of our equipment was pretty dated, scratched, dented and otherwise abused. George was our pole vaulter, which I always found amazing. You see, George was legally blind – although, I'm not sure there was such a term then. He had coke bottle glasses, and when he read, he had to have the book about an inch from his face. In spite of this handicap, he was a good student, not given to self-pity, with a good sense of humor.

I could never see (no pun intended) how he could run full tilt down a runway, carrying a twelve-foot-long pole in front of him, and find the box at the front of the pit to plant the pole. I had tried that event before, and knew what happens. As you pound down the runway toward the pit, the flexible pole begins to bend with every step, and it seems to have a life of its own. Then, as you reach the pit the pole must be lowered at just the right time, and into a very small space in the pit box so the pole will carry you straight up instead of off to the side. Assuming that goes well, when you reach the top you must push off from the pole at just the right moment and bend yourself over the cross bar, and (hopefully) over the pit. With all the jiggling and bouncing, and the pole bending back and forth with every step, I could never get the pole planted very well, and many times ended with some kind of disaster. So, I was very impressed with George's ability.

I know many of us felt the same way, and felt somewhat sorry that we didn't have one of those new, super flexible and strong fiberglass poles for George to use. Somehow, when the bus carried us home after the meet there was a new pole in the bus for George. Coach asked us about it. Nobody knew anything. Hmmm.

Drive Safely

As the time approached when we could get our drivers' licenses, my friends and I began to talk about how to act with a car, and how to go about asking to use the family vehicle. We concluded that it would be a good idea to decide every week or so what we really wanted to do, and just ask for the car at those times, rather than pestering our parents every day for the keys. That way, we would stand a better chance of getting the car when we actually wanted it.

That sounded like a grand plan, and I think it lasted about two weeks after I got my license.

We didn't have Drivers' Education at our school and there were no private instruction companies, so my dad taught me how to drive. When I got to be fourteen, I started pestering him to take me out on Sunday afternoons to learn. Once in a while he would take me to a lonely stretch of county (read gravel) road, and we would switch places. I know that a lot of my friends received a lot of cautions and instructions before starting that first driving effort, but not me. Dad just got into the passenger seat, closed the door and just sat there looking straight ahead. I loved my dad, but he was not a great communicator.

At that time, we had a 1956 Buick that Jerry had bought new while he was in high school (!!!) He had been working at the local weekly newspaper as a linotype operator, and had saved a lot of money. Sometime after he graduated he decided he wanted a convertible, and our 1951 Chevrolet was getting a little long in the tooth, so he sold his Buick to our parents.

It was a beautiful two-tone green four-door hardtop with whitewall tires and an automatic transmission. So, that's the car in which I learned how to drive.

I put the car in drive (D for Drag) and took off down the gravel road. We had stopped at the bottom of a small hill, and as we started up that hill the back end started bouncing around and making lots of noise. Dad didn't say anything, but I looked at him with concern on my face and asked, "What's wrong?!"

"You're going too fast!"

"Oh." As I took my foot off the accelerator (foot feed), I wondered why he hadn't said anything before but, oh well. Anyway, the car settled right down. *Huh! I was going too fast.* Fortunately, I didn't run into anything, and didn't commit any more foolish acts in front of him. We went out several more times, with the same lack of communication but with me getting more proficient each time.

I read the state information book for getting a driver's license, and when the time came I aced the written test and got my learner's permit. After that it was off to the races (almost literally). I passed the driving test with no problems, and now I was armed with most of the required weaponry for dating; the missing portion being enough money to buy gas and treat a lady.

I sought every opportunity to run an errand for my folks. I was driving downtown one day, just two weeks after getting my license, and

I saw Joe Dale walking toward his house. Here was an opportunity for me to show off, and to do a good deed at the same time. Joe Dale went to our church, and had a learning disability; most people liked him. I stopped and asked him if he wanted a ride home and he, of course, said yes. Just after I picked him up the street took a sharp, 90-degree left turn to head out to Parkway Village. I was going too fast again, the car slid in the gravel on the side of the road, and we went off the road and into a tree in someone's yard.

Joe Dale hit his head on the windshield and dashboard, and had a pretty good cut on his forehead. It was only a few blocks to our house, so I ran home and told Mom what had happened. She and I returned to the scene, and got there before the police arrived. The car was towed to our house and dropped in the back yard, until the insurance company adjuster came and evaluated it. They totaled it out and towed the car away, but before that happened I had to look at that beautiful wreck every day as I did my normal chores, and wonder what the Hell I was thinking when I took the curve that fast.

When the policeman came to take my information at the wreck he asked for my license and registration of course, and all I had to give him was the temporary paper copy, because my permanent copy had not come back from BMV yet. Didn't even have my permanent license copy yet, and I had already totaled our car!

Fortunately, Joe Dale was not seriously hurt and I had only minor bruises. Mom however, was a wreck. Dad on the other hand, took it in stride for some reason.

So, it was time to go car-hunting. Surprisingly, Mom took me along to pick out a new car. After looking at a lot of used cars, we settled on a 1959 Chevrolet with a standard transmission and straight-six engine. 1959 was the peak year for tail fins, and the '59 had beautiful, huge fins with teardrop rear lights. The car had fourteen-inch wheels and sat really low to the ground.

I loved that car. It was not only stylish, it would scream like a banshee. With the standard transmission, I could make it act like a really souped-up V8, until it reached top end. Unfortunately, none of my previous bad acts taught me anything and I continued to drive like a maniac.

I was fortunate in that all of the girls I dated were really nice people. Most were from my church, but several I just knew from school.

It was snowing – strange for late April in Missouri. It was a Sunday, April 22, 1962. I wanted to go to a show in Union (the theatre in St. Clair had closed by that time), but had no date. Typically, I did not plan ahead, and was just calling around to see if anyone was interested. My first choice was a girl I had noticed in the class behind me. Charlene was not interested. Drat! I really wanted to date her. Oh well, try somebody else for today. I called two or three other girls with the same result.

Mom asked me what was up, and I told her I was trying to find somebody to go to the show with me. She said, "Why don't you ask that nice Schroeder girl – what's her name?"

"Gail. Yeah, I could ask her. She has never seemed interested in me, though."

"Well, you won't know unless you ask".

So, I called the Schroeder house and asked for Gail. "Would you like to go to a movie this afternoon?"

"Sure, I would love to. What time?"

"I'll pick you up at 2."

"Okay, I'll be ready. Thanks for asking me."

"*Okay, I have a date!* You were right, Mom, she said yes."

"I thought she might." As it turned out, Mom and Mrs. Schroeder had been talking!

So, I drove the few blocks to Gail's house and picked her up. She was dressed in a pretty, light blue shirtwaist dress that really looked great on her. I walked her back to the car, got in behind the steering wheel and turned on the windshield wipers to clear the snow off. They made a couple of cycles and then turned off. We had a bad wiper motor or a bad connection, and it would just randomly shut off and then just as randomly turn back on. You never knew if the wipers were going to stay on or off for any particular time, so it was somewhat exciting in a downpour.

"Did you turn those off? I didn't notice that you did anything?"

"No, I don't have to turn them on and off – they are automatic. They sense when there is too much moisture on the windshield and turn on. Then when it gets dry enough, they turn off."

"Really?! Wow, this is some car. I never heard of that before."

"Yeah, it's an experimental thing. Almost no other car has it."

"Wow, that's really something!"

"Isn't it though? The rearview mirror is automatic too. When someone comes up behind you at night and their lights are too bright, it dims the mirror so you don't get blinded. Nobody else has one of those, either."

"Boy, this is some car!"

The story about the rearview mirror was true. Bob (my brother-in-law; married to Maxine) worked at the Guide Lamp Division of General Motors, and had been working on development of the self-dimming mirror. He had installed an experimental unit in our car and it was a new idea at the time. However, the story about the automatic wipers was a complete fabrication. Why did I do that? I have no idea. Did I need to do that to impress this new girl? No not really, and I don't think that was my motivation. I think I did it as a joke, thinking the idea was so preposterous that nobody would believe it, and we could have a good laugh. However, after she believed me, I couldn't really walk that back so I just left it there.

So much for honesty and integrity.

Anyway, we enjoyed the show, and she was even willing to date me again the next week. And so, a beautiful relationship began. I continued dating other girls for a short while, but it wasn't long before I decided that Gail was the girl for me. When I got my high school ring in the fall, I asked her to go steady and wear my ring, to which she agreed. My ring size was 10 and hers was 5, so she had to put about sixteen rolls of white tape around it so it would fit. Some girls did that, others wore their rings on necklaces.

So, we went steady through my Junior and Senior years. I would usually walk the mile or so to her house before school, and we would continue the walk to school together. Then we would walk the halls together until school started, and walk back home together after school.

In the summer, as I was delivering feed to, or picking up eggs from, farmers, I would usually take her with me in the pickup. We also found things to do together several nights every week, and she even started going to church with me on Sunday evenings. We became inseparable, and have stayed together all this time – what's wrong with her judgement, anyway?

Regular or Ethyl?

I was sitting in the old, wooden office chair behind the counter at the front of the feed store, wondering how I was going to make some date money. Girls had begun to be very important to me, and you couldn't make much of an impression by relying on the girl's parents to take you to church suppers, or drop both of you off at the movie theatre. No, a guy had to have his own wheels. It wasn't just gas money. You had to be able to show a girl a good time, like taking her to the drive-in, or out to eat at The Twin Bridges Truck Stop. Then there were dances at school, and ball games, and on and on.

Not that I minded working for Dad in the feed store. I had always been willing to do that, but he couldn't afford to pay me anything, and I knew enough not to ask. The feed and chicken business had been on a down spiral since 1945, and although the overall economy was doing pretty well in general, 1958 was not a good year. Auto companies had laid off a lot of workers, many of them from St. Clair. Small businesses were closing and a lot of people were out of work. Even farmers felt the pinch, as a lot of the smaller ones had been supplementing their farm incomes with other jobs which now did not exist.

A lot of Dad's customers bought feed and chickens on credit which Dad carried. By 1960, the amount of receivables (I didn't know that term then) he had on the books was more than his annual revenue. He couldn't say no to anyone. Eventually that was his downfall. He had to declare bankruptcy. Both Mom and Dad took extra jobs. Dad went to work pumping gas at Keys Twin Bridges Truck Stop, working nights, and Mom went to work at the shoe factory. So, I wasn't about to start asking my parents for money for dates. No, that just wasn't done. What to do.

"What are you so serious about?" Sherman came through the hall door, trailing smoke from his five-cent Phillies cigar. "You look like somebody just shot your dog. Are you ok?"

"Yeah, but I need to make some money. Could I work for you, maybe drive your truck, or help you pump oil and gas?" I did okay this past winter, when you were sick, didn't I?

"What happened, did your boss fire you from the paper already?"

"No, I'm still working there, but she only pays 75 cents an hour and I only get ten or twelve hours a week. That doesn't buy many movie tickets. I need to make some real scratch. You know that half a dozen guys in my class already have their own cars? I walk to school and here come these guys down the school driveway in their own cars, and you know what? Most of them have a girl in the car, too. To make matters worse, most of the girls in my class are going out with guys in the class ahead of me because they can all drive, and most of them now have cars. It makes the competition really tough."

Sherman blew several smoke rings and thought a minute. "I can't really use you, but I think I know someone who could."

"Really? Who would that be?"

More smoke rings. "He manages a gas station out on the highway. He wants to stay open all night and catch more of the evening traffic, but can't find honest help he can trust. I can put in a good word for you."

"Oh man, that would be great! How much does he pay?"

"You'll have to ask him, but I'm pretty sure it will be more than Dorothy's paying you. I'm going to make a run out there in a couple of hours anyway; I'll talk to him."

"That would be great. Thanks, Sherman."

Sherman stubbed out his cigar in the ashtray on the counter, left by the front door and climbed into the tank truck. As he drove off, my mind was racing. A job at a filling station on the highway. What could be better? I'll learn a lot about cars, I'll have this really neat job – out on the highway – and money will be pouring in. I'll be able to go out on real dates!

I felt so good about the possibilities that I decided I needed to learn how to blow smoke rings. I picked a Phillies out of the display box on the counter and lit it. I got a good fire going, and drew in a mouthful of smoke. I tried to do what I had seen Sherman do, and blew out a little smoke gently. Just a trail of smoke. I blew it all out, and drew in another mouthful. Ok, this can't be that hard. Just hold your mouth in an O, and blow gently. No, that didn't work either. After several more drags and puffs, I noticed I was getting a headache. Then I got dizzy, and had to sit down. Maybe this can wait till some other time. I put the cigar out, and sat in the chair holding my head. *My gosh, how can people stand this stuff?*

I sat there hoping nobody would come into the store for a while, because I didn't think I could stand up. Or, if I stood up, I might throw up. I was just beginning to feel a little better when I spotted her. Miss Crotchety was walking up the ramp to the store. She was wearing her trademark black suit, black broad brimmed bonnet, and holding her small black handbag under her right arm. It made her look as mean and fierce as she really was. She never failed to ruin everyone's day, no matter where she went.

"I want a dozen medium eggs. And I want them all white – no brown eggs."

"Yes, Ma'am." I walked to the medium egg case, and began to transfer a dozen eggs to an egg carton. Every egg had been weighed on a balance scale. The printing under the needle indicator was divided into four areas: small, medium, large and extra-large. Each area included a weight range, so the eggs within one of the classes could vary somewhat, but had to be a minimum weight for that class. After you had graded a hundred dozen eggs or so, you could divide most of them by sight. But if there was any doubt, the egg went on the scale.

As Miss Crotchety watched me, she tapped me on the shoulder. "Young man, some of those eggs are smaller than the others."

Without looking up or stopping, I said, "No Ma'am, some of them are bigger than the others." She huffed, and walked over to the counter and began digging in her purse for the money to pay for the eggs. I couldn't hear what she was saying to herself under her breath, but I'm sure it had something to do with the devil, final judgment, my ancestry, and such.

Dad came into the store about then and walked around the counter to see what I was doing. I finished making out the sales slip and turned the crank to roll it out of the machine, and said, "That'll be thirty-seven cents, please."

She had watched me write out the sales slip, and said, "A left-handed man is the devil's own workshop!" I knew I had pushed my luck with the first remark, so I just handed her the receipt and smiled. She counted out the thirty-seven cents, mostly pennies, and seemed to pinch every coin as she turned it loose as if she couldn't stand to part with it. I took the money, gave her a little smile, and thanked her.

Dad smiled and said, "Thank you Miss Higgins. Have a nice day." As she closed the door, dad said "Bitch! I don't think the devil could stand to be married to her." He was left-handed too. He patted my shoulder once, looked at the cigars in the ashtray, and sat down in the office chair. He was a man of few words.

Late in the afternoon, Sherman was back. It was all I could do to wait for him to come through the door so I could ask him. "Were you able to talk to the man?"

Ignoring me completely, with a wry grin on his face, he said, "Hello, Floyd. Pretty hot again today, wasn't it?"

"Yeah, I'm glad I'm working nights again. It's much cooler. The heat off that blacktop during the day just about does me in."

Sherman grinned devilishly. He knew I couldn't wait for the news; he was just yanking my chain. Turning to me, finally, he said, "Hanson said he will be in the station tomorrow morning, and for you to come in around 9 so he can talk to you. I lied, and told him you are a good kid. Don't make me look bad." Both Sherman and dad had a good laugh. Then dad's smile left.

"Are you thinking of working on the highway?"

"Well, I don't have the job yet. I haven't even talked to Mr. Haynes yet. I thought it would get me some more money. It would be the same kind of job you do at Twin Bridges Truck Stop, except his traffic is mostly cars."

"It can be dangerous on the highway. Have you told Mom about this yet?"

"No, Dad, I just thought of it today, and Sherman said Mr. Haynes is looking for help." Dad just shrugged his shoulders, and turned toward the desk. Man of few words.

The Interview

The next morning I put on a fresh t-shirt and clean levis, (that was business casual, in Missouri in the 60's) and drove the pickup (remind me to tell you about the pickup) to the gas station, arriving a few minutes before nine. I figured arriving late for a job interview would be a bad start. Mr. Haynes met me at the front door of the station with a "Good morning, what can I do for ya? Need some tires for that old truck?"

"No sir, my name is DeWayne Landwehr, and I came to see if I could get a job here. Are you Mr. Haynes? Sherman told me you might be able to use some help."

"That's me. Are you Floyd's kid?"

"Yes sir, that's my dad."

"You can cut the 'sir' stuff, my name is Hanson. Ever worked in a gas station before?"

"Well, not for money. I've spent several hours at the Twin Bridges Truck Stop helping my dad pump gas in the big trucks that come through there."

"Ever change a tire?"

"Sure, I've had flats on dad's car a few times."

"So, you know how to operate a tire jack, but have you ever put a new tire on a rim?"

"No sir."

"Hanson!"

"Okay, no I haven't, Hanson."

"Know how to operate a credit card machine?"

"No, I don't."

"Can you make change, at least?" (getting exasperated)

"Oh yeah, I work in Dad's store all the time and I can make change really well."

"Well, at least that's something. You've got two things going for ya, you know that? Sherman said you are okay, and you're Floyd's kid. I'll give you a try for a couple of weeks at $1.25 an hour, and if you work out then I'll give you a raise, maybe to $1.50. Depends on how well you do. Does that sound ok to you?"

"Oh yes sir, Hanson. That will be just fine."

"Okay, one more thing. We operate on commission here. You get fifty-cents for an air filter, a dollar and a half for a voltage regulator, two dollars for a generator, and five dollars for a new tire. Oh, and you also get four bits for a used tire. Any questions?"

"No, I've got it."

Okay, I'm going to show you how to use the credit card machine and operate the cash register, then I'm going to let Levi Richter show you the ropes around the station, the garage and the pumps."

In those days there was no internet, so the credit card machine was just a mechanical roller that you put the credit card and a charge slip on, then rolled the roller over it. That imprinted the card number on the charge slip, which was then hand written for the purchase. The credit cards were traded to the wholesaler (Sherman) for more gas the next time he came by to refill the storage tanks. The wholesaler then sent them on in similar manner to the parent company where they were finally processed for payment. Consequently, it could be a week or more before charges actually came through to the card.

Levi was your average, run of the mill Missouri redneck. He stood about five-ten and weighed about 230. He had a weathered, ruddy complexion and brown hair that he wore in the typical crew cut of the time. I don't think he owned a sports shirt. He always wore T shirts, but they had to have a pocket in them. I didn't know Levi, but he wasn't that much older than me, and had a reputation as somewhat of a wild child. While Levi didn't know me either, in this community everyone knew about every family, if not each individual member.

"Levi, this is DeWayne Landwehr—"

"You Floyd's kid?"

"Yes, I am."

"Levi, listen. We're going to see if DeWayne has what it takes to work here; give him a try for a couple weeks. I want you to show him around. Make sure he knows how to operate all the equipment, and where everything is."

Turning to me, he said, "DeWayne, if he thinks you'll work, you can start tomorrow at 9. You can work four hours a day for the rest of this week, then we'll work out a schedule to get you some more hours."

"I'm going to pick up Jackie and take the Harley out for a spin. I'll be back to check on you two later."

Hanson got into his pickup and drove down the gravel side road toward his house, trailing dust. It was only a few seconds before the dust rolling up behind the truck completely hid it from view.

Levi sized me up. It was pretty obvious that he was one of those who didn't much care for the Landwehr family. I had noticed ever since starting first grade that there were strong feelings about such things. People either liked you, based on your family, or they didn't. If they didn't, there was not much you could say or do about it. You just had to try to live with it, and hopefully things would work out. "How much do you know about working in a gas station?"

"You might as well start from the beginning. Hanson already asked me all those questions, and I didn't have very many good answers – but, I learn real quick." We walked back into the office just as Hanson and company came roaring back up the gravel road trailing dust, and rocketed out onto the highway. He had a beautiful crème and chrome Harley, with a windscreen, saddlebags and streamers from the handlebars. He and Jackie both were wearing leather jackets and boots, but no helmets (you just didn't wear a helmet then, if you were cool). Instead, he wore a biker's cap, and Jackie was wearing a scarf. They turned right out of the station and roared West on Route 66, streamers flying.

Levi showed me where the air filters were, and how to look up the right model for a specific car. Then we looked at the oil filters and went through the same routine with the cross-reference charts. Tires were in the lube room, and again there were charts with recommended tires for specific cars and trucks.

We were just getting into voltage regulators and generators when a customer pulled in and ran over the signal hose, ringing the bell to alert us we had a customer. "Okay, you take this one, and I'll watch to see how you do."

So, I walked out to the car and asked the driver of the '55 Chevy if I could help him. "Yeah, give me two dollars' worth of regular." So, I turned the crank on the pump to roll it to zero, turned the pump on, stuck the hose in the fuel filler, and pumped out about 8 gallons of gas (gas was selling for $0.259 then). When that was done, I took the two singles from the driver, and he drove off.

"How'd I do", I asked.

"Terrible. I don't know if you're going to work out or not. But, let's put the money in the cash register first, and then I'll tell you what you did wrong."

So, we walked into the office and he showed me how to ring up the sale, and use the key to open the cash drawer. Then he lit into me.

"DeWayne, the main idea here is to fuck da public!! You are never going to sell any accessories the way you approached that guy, and you won't sell as much gas, either. If you don't get with the program, you won't cut it here. We don't have many repeat customers; most of them are just traveling through and won't be back, so you have to skin 'em when they come in."

"When a customer comes in, you run out to the car – don't walk – and, you don't say, 'can I help you?' – you say, 'fill 'er up?' Sometimes people will pull in thinking of just a couple of dollars' worth, like that last guy. If you say 'fill 'er up' sometimes they will decide to get a tankful. Then, whatever their answer is, you say, 'will that be regular or ethyl?'"

"But, what if I already know that the car uses regular gas?"

"Listen to me, kid. Remember the 'main idea' I just told you about. Sometimes people will decide to give their car a treat. Other times, they won't know what to put in, and you can suggest that ethyl will be much better for their car. Get it?"

"Yeah, I got it."

About that time, Hanson and Jackie came roaring back on his crème and chrome Harley, stopped in front of the station by the Ethyl pump, and put the kickstand down. Jackie climbed off the back, and Hanson filled up the bike. Then he turned to Levi and asked, "Well, how did he do?"

"He has a lot to learn, but I think he'll be okay. I need to teach him a lot more stuff."

"Okay, DeWayne, why don't you come in around 8 O'Clock tomorrow morning, and work till noon with Levi here. Do that for the rest of the week, and we'll see how you work out."

We shook hands. "Thanks Mr. Haynes. I really appreciate it."

Later, I told Dorothy that I had found another job, and wouldn't be back. She wished me luck; I think she was actually relieved that I wouldn't be smoking up her shop and office anymore.

The Pickup

Dad had acquired a used truck that had been fitted with an old beer-truck body. Maybe the truck had been a beer truck at one time. It had dual wheels, sliding doors on the sides, and doors in the back. He used it to pick up feed and supplies in St. Louis, deliver feed and supplies to customers, take chickens and eggs to market, and other types of deliveries.

When I turned fifteen, I began pestering Dad to allow me to start the car when the weather was cold. I was thrilled if he agreed, and would happily sit in the frigid car with the engine running, and imagine how it would be when I could really drive. I got my learner's permit to drive, and began moving the truck around on our property when it needed to be moved from one location to another to load or unload something or other. It was amazing how many times I could think of a valid reason why the truck needed to be moved! A lot of this movement involved backing up to a dock or door to be accessed.

I had watched closely as Dad looked in the outside rearview mirror, or occasionally, opened his door and leaned out to look back as he backed up. I decided I had to try that, so the next time I needed to unload some feed at the battery house I put the truck in reverse and looked out the side window at the rearview mirror and backed up. After getting to what appeared to be close enough to the building, I put the transmission in neutral, engaged the "emergency brake", got out and walked to the back of the truck to see how I had done. I was still yards from the building. Not good. I got back in the truck and repeated those steps several times, only getting marginally closer, but not close enough. I could see the building alright, but judging just how close I was to it was a real trick.

Okay, it was time to try opening the door and leaning out to look directly back at the building. I put the transmission in reverse, opened the door, and realized this was going to be harder than it looked when Dad did it. I could lean out the door okay if I had my left foot on the running board, but I needed that foot to operate the clutch. So, I took firm hold of the door at the bottom of the open window, grabbed the steering wheel firmly with the other hand, leaned out for a look, and pitched out the door, almost falling onto the ground when I let out the clutch. As I was recovering from my near-exit from the vehicle, I heard an awful CRUNCH behind me. I had taken out part of the front wall of the building. '*Well, that should be close enough – crap!*' I shut off the engine and went around to unload the feed before I caused any more damage. I had a nice wide opening to walk through now.

Dad never chastised me for that, nor did he even mention it to me. Nevertheless, I was really upset with myself for damaging his property. I think I would have felt better if he had punished me in some way, but that was not his manner. What hurt me more than anything was the face he would make as he looked at yet another fiasco perpetrated by his second son, and grimaced. The lips would press tightly shut, his mouth would be in a frown, sometimes one eyebrow would go down and the other one up, and wrinkles would deepen around the top of his nose and above his eyes.

As the business wound down in the late 50s, the big truck became very expensive to operate as loads became smaller and smaller. So, he found a 1953 Chevrolet pickup that had been owned by an auto mechanic in town. The really cool thing about this pickup was that the engine was chrome plated! It was so cool to show off to my friends. It also had a standard transmission, (three on the tree) but I had already learned how to handle that with the big truck.

I usually drove the pickup to work at the gas station. If business was slow, I often pulled the truck onto the grease rack, and practiced lubricating it. I don't think the truck had ever had so much grease applied to it. I discovered that if I shut the engine off while the engine was running pretty fast, that it would backfire. How cool was that?

The next time I drove the truck to school (yeah, I now had a ride to school!), I was showing it off to Larry, Glenn, Gary and some others, and decided to show them the backfire trick. I knew that if I shut it off just right and turned it back on real quick, that the engine would backfire and then keep running. This time though, the resulting noise was deafening. I thought I had blown the engine up. Larry thought I had split the muffler. I shut it down immediately, and climbed out to assess the damage. When I looked under the hood, I could not see any apparent damage, but knew it could be hidden inside the engine. Larry looked under the truck at the muffler, and was fortunate that he was already on his back, because he was laughing so hard.

The front muffler clamp had not been very tight, and the backfire just blew the front of the muffler away from the exhaust pipe. It was a simple matter to just slide the muffler back onto the pipe, and everything was copacetic. Now I really had a toy! Cutouts, glass packs and Lakes pipes were really popular at the time, and every red-blooded teenager wanted a car that made a nice rumble. Now I could be driving around quiet as you please, and with a simple flick of the switch be blowing your windows out. I can tell you I had a lot of fun with that little trick.

Some days after my shift at the filling station (when I was working nights), I would help Dad by making small feed deliveries in the pickup. Gail was my steady girl by that time, and I would usually call her to see if she wanted to ride along. She almost always agreed, so I came to understand that she liked riding in the pickup. (It was not until many years later that she told me how she HATED it!)

One particular day, I had a couple of deliveries to make that totaled about 2,500 pounds. I threw all the bags in the back (half ton pickup), picked up Gail and headed out on gravel roads that were filled with potholes. As we hit one of those craters, the right leaf spring broke. There was a tremendously loud BANG, and the right side of the truck bed collapsed down onto the frame. I first thought I had a blowout, and then sensed the problem was something worse, as I brought the truck to a rapid halt at the side of the road. When I got out, I could see that the tire was still ok, and it took me a few seconds to figure out that the problem was a broken spring.

The truck was still drivable, so I continued to make my deliveries, although at a much more sedate and circumspect pace, attempting diligently to avoid any more potholes. After dropping Gail back home it was getting close to time for my next shift, so I drove the truck to work with the thought that perhaps it was repairable, if I could get the truck onto the lift.

"What the Hell happened to your truck?!" Levi was so smooth. I told him what had happened. "Pull it onto the lift. Maybe it's just a broken shackle bolt. That wouldn't be so bad."

I wasn't sure what a shackle bolt was, but it sounded pretty harmless to me. However, as we got under the truck and took a look, the problem was immediately apparent. The main leaf of the leaf spring, that contained the shackle bolt, had broken. That meant replacing the entire spring assembly.

"Go to the junkyard on 47 tomorrow and get a new one, and put it on tomorrow night. Did you say your girlfriend was with you when it happened?"

"Yeah, she was pretty scared. The noise was so loud, it scared both of us. We didn't know what had happened."

Levi grabbed his ample belly and had a really good laugh. "I'll bet she had to check her underwear, didn't she? You should have pointed out that the spring broke on her side!" He ripped off another long belly laugh.

"Yeah, that would have really helped our relationship. I don't think that would have been such a good idea."

The next day I went to the junkyard, got a replacement spring and brought it with me to work so I could replace it during my shift. I put it up on the rack, and looked to see what had to be done. The spring had broken just behind the front shackle bolt, so I took out the front bolt, and then took out the rear bolt. I hadn't realized that the rear bolt was still holding the bed above the frame somewhat, so when I hammered out the rear bolt, the whole bed dropped another couple of inches with a terrific bang. Of course, my head was right up in there and the noise and sudden movement scared the life out of me. I instinctively ducked down to avoid the bed as it came crashing down to sit on the frame and then had to pause for a bit, while my heart relocated from my throat back to my chest. Then I jacked up the bed, removed the old spring and replaced it with the new one I had bought. I was pretty proud of myself. What could have been a costly repair, had only cost me five dollars for the spring, and a new pair of underwear.

The Grease Rack

Cars today have lifetime-lubricated bearings, and few if any of the joints require lubrication. Cars of the 50s did not have such things, and it was common for them to have as many as 15 or 20 grease fittings, or zerks. There were no places to get a quick, fifteen-minute lube and oil change. Those were twenty years into the future. Nearly every filling station had a vehicle lift, referred to as a grease rack. Ours had a central air cylinder that powered the lift, and two horizontal rails onto which the vehicle was driven. There were upturned stops at the front end of the lift that stopped the vehicle from being driven off that end. As the lift was raised off the floor, hinged stops at the rear would raise up to keep the vehicle from rolling off the back end of the lift once it was in the air.

Levi taught me how to operate the lift, how to find most of the zerks, and operate the grease gun, so I began to perform lube and oil changes for customers. One day a customer rolled in and I pulled his car onto the lift for the now-routine operation. The car had a manual transmission which was no problem for me, but for some unknown reason I left it in neutral as I got out of the vehicle and operated the lever to raise the lift.

I also hadn't driven the vehicle all the way to the front end of the lift, so the center of gravity was somewhat rear of the center pillar. As the lift began to rise, the car rolled toward the rear. There would have been no problem if I had continued to raise the lift, because the rear stops would have stopped the car, but I panicked. Seeing the car start to roll to the rear, I envisioned it flying off the lift, dropping to the ground from six feet in the air, and rolling into the lot right into another car pulling in for gas, so I reversed the lift to lower it back to the ground. The lift reached the floor just before the car reached the rear stops. The stops automatically receded into the lift as it came down, and the car rolled off the lift just as I had imagined it would, right between the two pump islands and into the path of a car coming in for gas. Fortunately for me I was there alone, and the entering car was going slow enough to stop before being smacked by the runaway vehicle from the lift. I had to be embarrassed and explain to only one person, and he wasn't my boss. It was good that he also had a sense of humor, and we had a great laugh out of it, although my laugh was more than a little nervous. Fortunately for me, the customer whose car I was supposed to be lubricating was sitting in the restaurant next door having lunch, and didn't see the ruckus.

What, I didn't tell you about the restaurant? Well, let me tell you. In the next lot, to the west of the filling station, was a restaurant and motel named for the two brothers who owned it; Scully's. It was just like hundreds of other establishments along Route 66 in those days. A modern motor hotel with a few cabins out back, and a restaurant that included a few booths and a diner-type food counter with bar stools. I never ate there, because we really didn't get a lunch break. However, I did go over there to get their wonderful iced tea on hot days. They had the best sweet tea, and it slaked my thirst a lot better than the soft drinks we had in vending machines at the filling station.

First Test

A young man drove into the station in a white 1951 Chevy. Levi was watching me, so I ran out to the car. "Fill 'er up, sir?" "Yes, please." I stuck the pump nozzle into the tank on the left fender, and went to the front to raise the hood. I knew where the latch release was because my dad had once owned a 1951 Chevy. I checked the oil; it was full. What next? Oh yeah, check the fan belts. They looked ok. How about the air cleaner? I unscrewed the wing nut and lifted the top off. The filter element was oily and filthy. The young man had gotten out of the car to get a Coke, and saw what I was doing. "What's that?"

"This is your air filter. See how dirty it is? This could really cause you problems. You should replace it. *(My first accessory sale, maybe?)*"

"Oh, thank you for pointing that out. This is my mom's car. She died a few weeks ago and left it to me. I live in California, and she had lived in New York. I am driving it back home and don't know anything about cars, so I appreciate your advice. I've got a long way to go, and don't need any problems. Please do replace it."

I took the dirty filter element into the station and began looking down the shelves of air filter replacements, trying to find one that indicated it was for a 1951 Chevrolet. Levi came around.

"What are you doing?"

"Look at this dirty filter. I'm trying to find the replacement for it, and can't seem to find the right one."

Levi had to lean on the counter to keep from falling over. He held his stomach as he bent over with laughter. "That's an oil bath filter, you dipstick. There is no replacement for it. You just clean it out in gasoline and put it back on. Charge him $2.50, and we'll split it."

"I can't do that. I told him it needed to be replaced."

"Does he know any different?"

"No, he said he doesn't know anything about cars. This would be cheating him."

"You go into the lube room and clean that filter out, and charge him, like I said."

"But…"

"Listen to me real close, Landwehr. How do you like your job? You do as I said, or this is your last day."

Embarrassed at having been scolded again, I dutifully went to the lube room with the air filter dripping dirty oil. I really didn't like this situation; it went against everything I had been taught. Although I didn't know it at the time, I was getting a lesson in employer-employee relations, as well as adult-child relations. I was conflicted, and silently arguing with myself. This wasn't right, but especially back then, a well-mannered child didn't argue with an adult. And, jobs were hard to get. It didn't pay to argue with the one who could fire you on the spot.

I rinsed the filter in a pan of gasoline, and it looked as good as new. I took it out to the car and tried to put in back in place without the young man seeing me, but he was interested, and watched the whole operation. As I was tightening the wingnut back in place, he thanked me again. He paid for the gasoline, and $2.50 for the air filter, and drove off happy.

As I came back to the cash register, Levi said, "Okay, ring up the gasoline but not the filter. You keep $1.25, and give me $1.25."

I did as I was told. "Good", Levi said. "Remember the main idea here and keep looking for ways to sell stuff. By the way, didn't he need any oil, or fan belts?"

"No, the oil was full and the belts looked good. There were no cracks in them."

"Alright, I'll wait on the next customer, and you watch me."

Levi ran out to the next customer and asked the usual question. The customer wanted a fill-up. After sticking the nozzle into the tank, he ran around to the hood, lifted it and pulled the dipstick out. Ripping the shop rag out of his back pocket, he quickly wiped off the oil and reinserted the dipstick into the holder until it stopped. As he did so, I could see that he had inserted his forefinger between the holder and the stop on the dipstick, so it appeared to the driver that he had indeed shoved it all the way down. The effect though, was to leave the dipstick raised up about three eighths of an inch. He pulled the dipstick back out and examined it. He carried it around to the driver and said, "It looks like you are a quart low, sir. You really should put in a quart."

The customer was grateful. "Oh my, thank you, yes, please add a quart of 10W30."

"Right away, sir!"

With that, he reached to the oil rack which sat between the pumps, and inserted a spout into one of the cans of 10W30, took off the filler cap on top of the valve cover, and dumped in the oil. As the oil was draining into the engine, he reached down to check the fan belts. Grabbing one with three fingers, so that his thumb and second finger were below the belt, and his index finger was above the belt, he bent the belt so that the 'v' section cracked a little bit. He called out to the customer, "Sir, you might want to take a quick look at this."

The driver got out of his car, and walked around to the front. "Look at this fan belt, sir, it's liable to break any time. You should really think about having it replaced."

"Good Lord, I had no idea! Can you replace it for me?"

"Sure, we can handle that for you. It will only take a couple of minutes."

"Okay, go ahead and do it then. Thanks for catching that. I have a long way to go this week. I'm driving all the way to California, and don't want anything to go wrong."

"That's a wise decision, sir. We'll have it going in just a couple of minutes."

He removed the now empty oil can from the engine and replaced the oil filler cap, then ushered me into the office. "See how easy that is? Now, can you find the right fan belt? It's a 1956 Mercury." I checked the cross-reference chart, and found the right fan belt. "Good, now you put it on."

I must have given him a questioning look, because he said, "All you need is a 9/16 wrench, and a pry bar."

I found the wrench and pry bar, and we went back to the car. He showed me how to loosen the two bolts that held the generator to the mounting bracket, and slide the generator along the bracket slot until the belt was loose enough to remove. Then I removed the old belt and put on the new one. I then slid the generator back along the slot, and inserted the pry bar between the engine and generator to apply tension to the belt. Then, with the other hand, I tightened the two bolts. The driver paid the bill, and drove off happy as a clam at high tide.

"See how it's done? I expect you to be doing that with every customer now. Hear me?"

"Yeah."

"Okay, I'm going home. You hold down the fort."

I tried to do what he wanted, but my heart wasn't in it. I could rationalize the air filters, because that had an effect on gas mileage and engine performance, but the oil levels and fan belt pinching were dishonest, and I could not bring myself to do that. Fortunately for me, cars at that time used enough oil and went through enough fan belts that I could show some sales for those items without cheating about it.

I guess Mr. Haynes was satisfied enough with my performance that he decided to hire some more teenagers in the station. Eventually, three more of us from the same class were hired. As people were added, I had some hope that I might be recognized as something of a leader of the group, since I had been hired first, and had the most experience. However, all three of the 'newbies' had more enthusiasm for the accessory sales than I did. Hanson soon gave me what was to be not the last lesson in humility I would ever receive, when he told me that I <u>and</u> my good friend Ron would share the small raise and slightly increased responsibilities of straw boss.

I didn't fight it or try to defend myself mostly because in those days, and in our neighborhood, you didn't argue with seniority or authority. Also, I knew I wasn't able to comply enthusiastically with Hanson's wishes, and the other three had far surpassed me in accessory sales and commissions. I just couldn't do it in good conscience.

Night Shift

One of the perks of being deemed leader was preference for day shift. We worked 12-hours shifts; 6 to 6. Since Ron and I were deemed to be 'equal', we alternated working the night shift every few weeks, in the summer time.

Day shift went sort of like this. Early morning and evenings, people were driving to work or home. If they stopped, they just wanted a fill-up – quickly. No nonsense, not much small talk, just fill up and go. During the middle of the day it was tourists. Again, a quick fill up, but they also wanted the windshields clean, oil checked, etc. Occasionally, there would be a flat tire to change, or an overheated radiator to cool off.

One very hot day, a lady stopped in in a cloud of steam and got out of her car almost in hysterics, after turning off the engine. I found the hood latch and lifted the hood to a giant hissing sound and a very hot sauna. I twisted off the radiator cap, and my wrist and lower arm were immediately parboiled. I had first and second degree burns from my fingertips part way up my arm. Levi came running over and turned the hose on my arm to cool it off; probably saved me from having worse blistering.

"You idiot! NEVER open an overheated radiator like that without a shop towel around your hand, and without the engine running. Have the car pull over here to the water hose, and tell them to leave the engine running. Then spray water on the radiator for a while to cool it down a little before you even touch it. Then just turn the cap to the first stop to slowly release pressure without spraying yourself with steam. Then remove the cap and add water."

That was a good lesson, because there were always overheated cars coming in during hot summer days. If that had happened during the night shift when I had been there alone, I would have been in trouble.

Sometimes there was a radiator leak that could be fixed with some Stop Leak, or a broken radiator hose that needed to be replaced. Most often however, the car owner had just not kept track of coolant levels, and had let the radiator run out of water. In those days, there were no 'puke tanks' like there are today, so the only way to add coolant was to remove the radiator cap and add it directly to the radiator.

One of the more interesting aspects to working in the filling station was meeting all the different people who came in. One summer day a family came in for a fill up, and to use the bathrooms. When I finished filling the tank and rang up the sale, the man walked out to his car and drove off. Nothing unusual in that, and I turned to wait on the next car. A couple of minutes later, the wife came around the corner and noticed the car wasn't at the pump. "Where's my car?"

"Which car were you in, Ma'am?"

"A blue Pontiac."

"Oh, I believe he drove off a couple of minutes ago."

"Oh my God, were the kids in the car?"

"Yes they were."

"Ohmygodohmygodohmygod! What am I going to do?!"

Ron was working with me that day and I think he smelled a reward coming. He turned to her and said, "Get in my car, we'll catch up to him."

Without hesitating she jumped into Ron's car and they sped off heading west. Ron was driving a 1959 Chevrolet with a six-cylinder engine, like ours. It would only do 105 miles per hour flat out, but he held it to the floor for several miles and finally caught up to the guy.

"There he is! That's our car." Ron pulled up beside the guy and honked his horn to get his attention. The wife had the window down and was waving frantically at the other driver. He acknowledged their presence, slowed down, pulled off to the side and stopped. The woman got out of Ron's car and entered the passenger side of the other car. Ron had gotten out of his car to talk to the husband. Ron told me later that the guy not only did not offer him a reward, he seemed somewhat put out that Ron had brought his wife to him. Wonder what was going there?

During the day there were usually two, and sometimes three of us working to handle all the traffic at the pumps and in the garage. On the night shift though, there would just be one person on duty. Not only was there less traffic during night shifts, but the traffic was from a completely different universe.

During the summer I worked seven days a week, but during the school year I just worked weekends. If I happened to be on days, that meant Saturday only, because I had to be in church as the organist on Sunday. If I was on nights however, that meant Friday and Saturday night. That was pretty grueling, as I had to report to work at 6PM Friday after school, work till 6 Saturday morning, when I went home and usually drove a truck for either my brother or father. I would try to see Gail at some point on Saturday, sometimes taking her with me on deliveries. Then I worked Saturday night, came home on Sunday morning, took a bath and went directly to church or the radio station, where our quartet might be singing. On Sunday afternoon, Gail and I usually went to a show, or just drove around. So, except for a catnap of an hour or so here and there, I didn't sleep from Friday morning until Sunday night.

One winter evening I was alone in the station when one of the "night tourists" (a hitchhiker) came strolling in, looking for a place to warm up. He looked pretty ragged and dirty, but not too much unlike many others I had seen before, so I didn't think too much about it. Until another showed up a few minutes later, and then another and another and another. Now, I was getting nervous. There were five of them, one a woman, and they were all together, even though they had tried to disguise that fact by coming in a few minutes apart.

I was wearing a hooded sweatshirt with a large pocket in front, so I went to the lube room and retrieved a large crescent wrench and stowed it in my pocket. If they wanted to rob me, I was not going to make it easy. They separated so I could not keep an eye on all of them at once, so I paced back and forth between them. I struck up a conversation with one of them, and found that they were part of a traveling circus, and had been left to their own devices to get to their next venue. That was their story anyway, and I took it with a grain of salt.

After a couple of hours, they finally left and I was greatly relieved. The good thing was that it had given me something to do for a couple of hours, and helped me to stay awake.

Staying awake was my primary focus on nights. I was usually fine until about two or three. Then it was a fight for consciousness until the sun came up. There was always a steady but slowing stream of customers until midnight, then it would be just a customer every now and then. As the amount of traffic ebbed and all other surrounding activity ceased, the quiet became almost palpable. I could hear the steady and mesmerizing hum of tires on individual cars as they approached and then passed by. Then there would be the heavy diesel popping as a truck motor-braked down Coal Mine hill, followed by the piston pounding as it roared up the next slope. One night, I heard the distinctive roar of a car with either glass packs or cut-outs approaching at high speed. My curiosity aroused, I walked out of the station toward the highway so I could get a better look at whatever was coming. From the rapidly changing pitch, I could tell that he was approaching at a pretty good clip. Within a minute the car came into view going West. It was a beautiful blue or turquoise 1959 Chevrolet with Lakes Pipes. He was traveling well over 100 miles per hour, and blue flames several feet long were shooting out of his pipes. He went around the curve and was gone in just a few seconds. I stood there for a few minutes or so and listened as the sound faded, then turned to go back into the station. It seemed like just a few minutes went by and I heard the car coming back, going even faster this time, and trailed by a State Police car. Later, a customer told me he had seen the car pulled over around Pacific, about thirty miles east. I'm sure the policeman just wanted to tell the guy what a great car he had.

Fort Leonard Wood was about fifty miles west of the station, so we were about half way between the fort and St. Louis. On Friday nights, some of the soldiers from the fort would get liberty for the weekend, and most would go to St. Roberts, a small town just west of the fort, for sex and alcohol. Those lucky enough to have access to transportation would head to St. Louis for the same reasons. In either case, they had to be checked back in to the fort by midnight Sunday.

The mad dash back to the fort usually started about 10PM Sunday night. We were about an hour from the fort, so those that came through at that time were usually drunk, but in no particular hurry. However, as time passed, the groups became drunker and more frantic – a very bad combination. By 11PM, those who stopped in for gas just wanted a dollar's worth; enough to get them to the fort. After 11 it was almost humorous to see the change. At this point, all in the cars were usually totally wasted, and resigned to being AWOL and subject to punishment, so while they were in somewhat of a hurry, they knew their goose was cooked anyway so they would usually have the tank filled, if they had any money left. One guy came in and only had a quarter, so he got just a gallon of gas. Almost always, there were a few who continued to dribble (almost literally) through until morning. Although they were mostly very drunk, they were never any trouble, and I didn't worry at all about them.

New Additions

Hanson loved to sell air filters and fan belts, but he REALLY loved to sell tires, as that was where he made the most money. He usually kept an inventory of about 75 tires (remember, this was a small station), but decided to upgrade. He suspected that if he had a wrecker, he could snag a lot more tire sales, so he bought a used one. Did I say used? I meant REALLY used. But it was red, for easy visibility, and he parked it right out front where everyone could see it. Before long, he had a wrecked car that he had towed in which he parked right behind it, but in front of the fuel pumps so everyone who came in could see it. When that one was towed away by the insurance company or whomever, he had another one to take its place.

A customer would come in and notice the car. "Wow, that car is a mess. Must have been some wreck." The car was a station wagon, with luggage strewn haphazardly throughout the car, the obvious result of a very bad wreck.

"Yeah, it's a really sad story, that one. A preacher came in last week with his family; wife, two little kids - and a cute little dog. I told him he had a bubble on his tire, about like that one on your left front there, and that he needed to change it before it blew out. You know, tread separation in this heat is a real problem, especially when you're going 70 miles an hour. He didn't take my advice, and just a couple of miles down the road, sure 'nuff, the tire blew. The car went off the road, down one of those steep embankments we have around here, hit some trees and killed them all. It was really ugly – and so unnecessary."

"Oh my God, those poor people…. You say I have a bubble on my tire? I don't see it."

"They're hard to see, but I look at this stuff every day and I can tell. That tire could be trouble."

Wife speaks up. "Fred, if he says we have a bad tire, we better have it changed. We have a long way to go."

"Okay, okay. Can you change a tire here?"

"Sure, and we have your size in stock – but, do you want to take a chance on the other three? They're the same make you know. Besides, you don't want to have an odd tire on your car, do you?"

And so it would go. In a lot of cases, the unsuspecting driver would be the proud owner of four new tires before he knew what happened. Then later, the old tires would be sold as used tires to someone else. In fact, this was working so well that before long he was having trouble keeping inventory in stock, so he took a bold step – he bought an entire tractor trailer load of tires at one time. We had tires stacked outside by the pumps, in the office so that there was just barely room enough to walk to the cash register, in the attic space over the station, and even the lube room was stacked floor to ceiling and wall to wall with tires. For a while, we could not use the lift for lube jobs, because it was completely blocked and stacked full. Within just a couple of weeks, enough tires had been sold that the lift was available, and by the end of summer, the entire inventory had been sold. The bright spot in all of this was that the locals suddenly had a ready source of inexpensive, but mostly still in good shape, used tires.

Me and J Edgar

Dad rarely ventured to give me advice on anything, but when I started working at the filling station, the one thing he warned me about was not to buy anything off the highway. Although he didn't bother to explain why, I knew that he was telling me that anything offered for sale by someone just passing through could very well be stolen.

Like all teenagers, I knew way more than my dad, so I took his advice with a grain of salt. I mean really, what would be the harm in buying a trinket now and then?

I was a sometimes coin collector. Not serious; I just loved to collect liberty dollars, Indian head pennies, Mercury dimes and stuff like that. When someone came in and paid with one of those things, or a silver certificate, or a two-dollar bill, I would trade it out of the cash register for some of my mundane currency. Sometimes I would ask them if they had any more of those things, and often they would, so I would buy them.

One evening during my normal night shift, a guy came through with a car full of novelties and trinkets. He offered to sell me several cartons of tax-free (read contraband) cigarettes, but I declined. I did however, buy a pair of those humongous sunglasses that are about three times as wide as your face. I thought those were cute, and what was the harm? He said he was a dealer, and I believed him. Who knows, maybe he was. Thus emboldened, I began to think that my dad had been a little overanxious in his advice.

One day a young man not much older than me came walking into the station. He had a flat tire just a mile or so down the highway, and didn't have a spare. Could I help?

What an opportunity! I could take the wrecker out. (What's a CDL?) I got in the wrecker and careened out of the station, turning right to the side road before entering the highway. As I did so, the force of the turn propelled me almost completely out of the cab. See, the door latch didn't really work, and so the door swung open as I turned. Fortunately, I had the window down and my arm resting on the door with my elbow out the window like any other really cool mechanic. I was able to put my foot on the running board and keep myself from falling completely out of the truck, and with some difficulty pulled myself back in and hit the brake. Okay, enough shenanigans.

More slowly now, I pulled onto the highway and drove to his car. I jacked the car up, took the tire off and threw it onto the wrecker and headed back to the station. I tried to sell him a new tire, but he said he just wanted that one repaired. I put a patch on it and we took it back to the car, reinstalled it on the car, which was a really beautiful red and cream 1955 Chevy convertible. Then we both drove back to the station where he got a full tank of gas.

Then I hit the jackpot. He didn't have enough paper money to pay for the service call, tire repair and gas. However, he did have a sack full of silver dollars and a transistor radio. Think of it – a transistor radio! I knew they existed, but had never had one of my own. He offered them in trade. Twenty-five Liberty silver dollars, a few two-dollar bills and the radio. I bought them all.

Until that time, the only radio we had in the house was a table model that had a broken Bakelite case, so all the tubes were visible. It had a faulty ground, so when you tried to tune it, you would get a shock as you turned the dial. There weren't that many stations we could get anyway, so it usually stayed tuned to the local station, KLPW, or to the St. Louis station, KMOX.

But now – now, I had a radio of my own – with 9 transistors yet. It was about the size of a pack of cigarillos, with a nice black carrying case that had a strap you could loop around your wrist for easy carrying. And, I could find some stations that were playing new music. Some people were beginning to call it Rock and Roll, but it was still usually listed as Rhythm and Blues on most music boxes. I was really proud of that radio and showed it around to everyone – except at home, because I knew dad wouldn't approve of how I got it.

A few weeks later, as I was in the feed store helping out, Dad came in and said, "Did you buy a radio off the highway?" *How did he know that?* I thought of denying it, but I could see the jig was up so I admitted it. He said, "You are in big trouble. They want you to come out to the station and bring the radio. You need to be there at 2 O'clock."

I was a little confused. I told him that Hanson had known about the radio, and didn't have a problem with it. He said, "It's not Hanson that wants you out there. It's the Texas Rangers."

"What?! Texas Rangers? What do they have to do with a radio?" I thought of saying something about Tonto and silver bullets, but something told me this was not the time to try out my twisted humor on dad.

"I don't know, and it really doesn't matter, does it? I told you not to buy anything off the highway, and you didn't listen. Now, get your butt out there, and don't forget the radio."

I retrieved the radio and drove out to the station. I parked dad's pickup at the side of the station and walked in, not really knowing what to expect, but suspecting I would be met with some sort of storm. Hanson was there, but nobody else. "I thought the Texas Rangers were here. What's going on?"

"They called from St. Louis a few hours ago, and asked if someone fitting your description worked here. Their description fit you perfect, and I told them 'yes'. Then they asked about a portable radio, so I told them I would ask you to bring it if you had it. I see you do. Did you buy it from some kid?"

"Yeah, dad always told me not to do that but I couldn't resist, and he needed the money to pay his bill."

"Well, they should be here pretty soon. They were leaving St. Louis when they called."

"Did they say what's going on? Why is Texas law all the way up here about a silly radio?"

"They wouldn't give me any more information. They just said to have you here by 2 O'clock."

I waited anxiously by the front window, watching for the cavalry to ride up any minute. After what seemed to be an eternity, a dark Ford sedan pulled up to the front door. Inside, the driver appeared to be a very serious body-builder type, with a flat top haircut and wearing a suit. In the passenger seat was an older gentleman, also in a suit, and in the back seat was the young man from whom I had bought the radio.

The driver exited the vehicle, and walked straight to Hanson. "Are you the owner here?"

"Yes, I am." Hanson's cheeks had turned red; he was embarrassed, and I think a little angry that the law had been called in on his establishment.

Turning to me, "Are you the young man who bought the radio?"

"Yessir." I am sure my cheeks, and also my ears, were red as well. I know they were burning. As I was standing there, I also had thoughts of horses and ten-gallon hats, and indeed, he was wearing a Stetson.

"Is that the lad you bought the radio from in the back seat?"

I had seen him in the car as they had driven up. "Yessir." I was dying to know what was going on, but too petrified to ask. The Ranger nodded to the gentleman in the front seat. He got out of the car, came in and shook my hand.

"How much did you pay for the radio, son?"

"$20, sir." He wrote me a check for twenty dollars, walked back out the door and got back in the car.

The Lone Ranger then turned to me again. "You know son, he didn't have to do that. Buying stolen property is a crime, and that property is subject to confiscation without compensation."

"yes sir, I know. But..."

He cut me off. "I'm pretty sure you didn't know the radio was stolen, but that makes no difference. It's still stolen property, and you have no rights to compensation. In fact, you could be sent to jail for it. Mr. _____ has insisted that nobody be prosecuted, and I am complying with his wishes, so I have not alerted your county sheriff. But make no mistake; you could have been in trouble for this."

I had never been so humiliated. All I could do was to hang my head, and say, again, "yessir."

"I don't owe you anything, but you seem to be a nice young man, so I want to make sure you take this lesson seriously. I am going to tell you how this whole escapade unfolded.

"That gentleman in the car had a son. The son's best friend is sitting in the back seat right now. The son died a couple of years ago, and the father was understandably devastated; it was his only child. The father decided to keep his son's memory as close as possible, so he kept the son's bedroom the same as the day he died. His Chevrolet convertible was kept in the garage under cover. He cleaned that car every week.

"A few weeks ago, that best friend broke into the house and stole most of the son's personal possessions. He packed them in the car, and took off. Of course, the father discovered the theft right away. He called us at the Texas Police Headquarters, and we began the search for the thief. Mr._____ insisted on going with us on the search, to recover all his son's personal possessions. He did not want anyone else to suffer due to this theft, so he intended to buy back everything we could find. We have been following the thief for over a week now, stopping at every gas station along the way, tracing his progress and buying back what we could find. We caught up with him in St. Louis yesterday, and are now retracing his route back to Texas. He is telling us where he stopped, and we are continuing to buy back things along the way. The convertible is being shipped back to Texas. I hope you know how lucky you are. Mr._____ could have pressed charges."

"Yes sir, I know. Thank you."

"Don't thank me. If it were up to me, you would be in trouble right now. Thanks go to him."

He turned, got back in the car and drove away. I felt wilted and drained. That poor man!

It was only a few weeks after that, that another black sedan pulled up in front of the station. I thought, *Oh, crap, now what? Did that man decide to press charges after all?* A man got out of the front passenger seat, who could have been the Texas Ranger's twin, with dark suit, flattop haircut, and all – except he wasn't wearing a Stetson. He approached me, and I was thinking, *Please, could I call home first before you take me in.* He held up a photo of someone and asked me if I had seen him. *Whew! It's not about me!!* "He would have been driving a red Pontiac. He probably would have come through here in the last couple of days. Did you see either him or the car?"

"I see hundreds of cars every day, but I don't remember seeing him. What did he do?"

"I can't tell you that. If you see him, please don't approach or try to apprehend him. Just call the me at this number." He handed me a business card with his name on it and the telephone number for the FBI field office in St. Louis.

Wow! The FBI! The closest I had ever been to law enforcement, until my run-in with the Texas Rangers a couple of weeks before, was to say 'Hi' to our neighbor, who was the town marshal; Marshal Wells. Now, within the space of just a few weeks, I was being accosted by all kinds of high-powered G-men.

Temptations

On the east side of the filling station was another motel, called the Skylark. It was a reputable place, but occasionally there were people who only wanted a room for a few hours (wink, wink).

There was a young woman who lived somewhere down the side road between the station and the Skylark. Just a few weeks after I had started working at the station, she drove up to one of the pumps. I ran out to service her car.

"Fill 'er up, Ma'am?"

She looked very Irish, with sandy reddish hair and a face full of freckles. She was wearing a flower-print, shirtwaist dress. The hem had been pulled up past her knees. "I don't need any gas. I've got a case of cold beer in the back. If you would get a room at the Skylark, we could have a party."

"Uhhhh, I'm working here by myself, and I can't leave."

"Well, when do you get off? Just get a room, and I'll wait."

"I really can't do that, Ma'am. I have a steady girlfriend."

She casually pushed her dress up a little farther on her thighs. "She doesn't need to know."

"No Ma'am, I guess she doesn't, but I would know. I really can't do that."

"Okay, but you're missing a really good party. I could show you a really good time."

"Thanks anyway."

I could tell she was not used to being turned down. She got a disgusted look on her face and sprayed gravel everywhere as she sped away.

Later, when Mr. Haynes came in to check on things, I told him what had happened, and asked if he knew her, because he lived down that same road somewhere.

"Oh yeah, that's Doris. You don't want to mess with her; you'll get more than you gave."

"What does that mean?" (Come on, give me a break. I was only 17, and a staunch Southern Baptist to boot).

"She'll screw anything that walks or crawls. She's been here a hundred times before. She was at a party a few years ago, and humped seven guys. She ended up pregnant, and one of the saps owned up to the job, and married her. She persuaded him to enlist in the army, and he's stationed in Germany. His enlistment was up last year, and she wrote him to re-up. She's collecting his dependents' pay, and doesn't want him back, but can't give up the sex. I don't know for sure, but I would bet she's not clean. She's got to have some kind of VD."

"Wow! Glad I didn't take her up on the offer."

"Yeah, I would steer clear of that."

Later, when Melvin came in to relieve me for the night shift, I told him about Doris.

"You idiot! Why didn't you take her up on that!?"

"It wouldn't have been right. You know I'm going steady. Besides, Hanson said she sleeps with anything that breathes."

"Well, I'll tell you one thing. If I get the chance, she won't have to ask me twice."

Sometime later, I was working the night shift, and Melvin drove up in his 1937 Plymouth pickup, with a canvas tent stretched across the back, and put a couple gallons of gas in his truck.

"Hey Melvin, where you goin'?"

"Goin' campin'. Meramec State Park. We're gonna' have a really great weekend."

I looked in the truck. There was Doris – and Lennie, too. "Did you get a cabin?"

"Naw, we're going to stay in the bed of the pickup. See, I got it all fixed up."

I looked in the bed. Under the canvas were a couple of rolled up blankets, and some cases of beer. "Yeah, looks like you're stocked up for the weekend."

"See ya later, chump."

With that, he jumped back in the truck and rolled out west toward the state park.

As I watched him leave, I continued analyzing my own feelings about the whole 'Doris' thing, as I had been doing since I had first met her a few weeks before.

I knew I had done the right thing, but why was it the 'right thing'? What did I want my life to be like; what kind of person did I want to be? What did I want other people to think of when they thought of me? One word kept coming back to me as I thought about those questions: Integrity. That's the word that I wanted people to think of when they thought of me. Oh, there were other words that I wanted to be associated with me, like honesty, kindness, good, etc., but Integrity was becoming my watchword.

So, it was beginning to come together for me. I had done the right thing, and now I was beginning to form concrete reasons for my behavior. But, there were some things I had to change about myself if I were to be true to my new watchword. I would have to buck some of the practices in the station, for one thing. I didn't have to make a big deal about it; I just wouldn't participate in them.

More Night Work

It was another long night. I had already cleaned the restrooms, swept the office and tidied up the lube room. There was hardly any traffic, and I was really beginning to feel sleepy. It was about 2AM, the worst time of the night for staying awake, and I decided to just sit down in the office chair for a minute and rest my aching feet. The next thing I knew, something was waking me from a dead sleep. I sat up and saw a man walking out of the station back to his car. He got in and drove off, looking back to wave at me as he left. I was really scared. What had he done while I was asleep? Had he stolen some gas, some tools, the cash from the cash register? Then I looked down and noticed two dollars laying on the desk. I ran out to the pump where his car had been, and the pump indicated $2 worth of gas had just been pumped.

Fortunately, that guy was one of the few regulars that came into the station periodically on his way to work. I could have been in real trouble, or worse. I thought about that as I drove home that morning, which happened to be Saturday. I don't think I ever fell asleep again at the station.

When I got home, around 7 Saturday morning, my brother Jerry needed for me to make a delivery for him. The delivery was about fifteen or twenty miles away, at a really remote farm, and I was not totally familiar with the location. It had been snowing; the roads and fields were snow-covered, but not too slick. I was almost to my destination when I suddenly awoke to the van bouncing along in the middle of a field. I had gone to sleep again, and run off the road. Fortunately for me, there was no ditch there, and no fence around the field I was in. The only way I knew how to get back to the road was the line of utility poles that I knew ran along the edge of the road. I turned back to those, and soon found the road again, but was once again shaken. There must be a purpose for me – twice within a few hours, that I could have been a lot worse off; either badly injured or dead.

Indian motorcycles

In spite of the fact that I sometimes suffered from lack of sleep, I rarely wanted to go home. Before I started driving, and when I was seeing girls with whom I could walk to the movies or just around town, there were many times that I did not immediately return home after walking the girl home, or after the end of an Explorer Scout meeting. I would wander around town, not really doing anything; there was nothing open in town after about 8PM. St. Clair was one of those towns people talk about when they say that 'they roll the sidewalks up' after dark. Oh, there was plenty of night life in the road houses scattered in remote areas around, but I was too young for that and besides, that was never my style.

Many times I would return home to find the house dark and locked up. I did not have a house key at the time, but I was not about to wake up either of my parents just to let me in. I decided to walk around to the back porch, to see if the back door was locked. If it was, I would just sleep on the porch until someone woke up in the morning, and I could walk in.

During the summer, my parents would often leave the back door open to provide a breeze through the house, and just hook the screen door. I discovered that if I pulled on the screen door just a little bit to provide a small amount of tension on the hook, and rapped the door lightly at the height of the hook, that it would jump right of the eye and I could walk right in and re-hook the door without waking anyone. That worked like a charm, and I used it many times to get home without notice. I just took my shoes off and tip-toed up the stairs to my room without anyone being the wiser.

After I began driving, I had a housekey, but I still didn't want to go home. I would drop off my date and instead of going home myself, I would drive around for a while, exploring roads and places I wasn't familiar with, and quite often would end up at the gas station. I would stop in and talk with whomever was there and drink a couple of cokes. The person working would usually be grateful to have someone to talk with and help them to stay awake. I would usually decide to hang it up and finally go home around two or three.

One of my favorite people to talk with was Bill. Bill was only about 4-1/2 feet tall, and worked the night shift as a second job to support his family of six kids. The funniest thing about Bill was his day job; he worked at the St. Louis Baby Carriage Factory. All kinds of one-liners and zingers went through my mind, but I never made fun of Bill, either to his face or behind his back.

First of all, he had arms like nail kegs, and could have made mince-meat of me without breaking a sweat. But more than that, he was a wise and sincere person that I came to respect a great deal. We talked a lot about family, right and wrong, being a good person, and he never lectured me. Our discussions were meaningful, and I came to look forward to them when he was working.

Bill rode an old Indian motorcycle. It wasn't restored, but looked almost new. He obviously took very good care of it. I really wanted to ride that bike, and pestered him a few times about that. He never really said no. Once, he said, "You think you might wreck it?" Of course, I said no I surely wouldn't, but it caused me to think. He just let that thought hang there and let it drop, and so did I.

Where's the Gas Tank?

No self-respecting male teenager would admit that he didn't know what model a car was, just by looking at it. One had to at least be familiar with the last ten years' models of the Big Four (General Motors, Ford, Chrysler and American Motors). Still hanging on was Studebaker, with its strange-looking cars, and there were some DeSotos, HenryJ's and Packards still around. There was no real foreign car presence in the US at that time. There were a few Austin-Healys, Triumphs and Jaguars, but not much else – at least, not in the Midwest. Every once in a while, one would see a SAAB (that funny-looking car that has the drive line to the front wheels instead of the back like everyone else), Volvo, or Volkswagen Beetle or microbus, but not often. No, it was just the American cars that interested us then.

During World War II, people could not buy cars, as all production capacity and resources had been devoted to the war effort. Consequently, there was a lot of pent-up demand for cars after VJ Day. Carmakers changed over all their plants from making tanks, airplanes and guns back to making cars. In the early days of vehicle production, automakers would introduce a model, and make it until a need for updating or change was perceived. After the war though, automakers gradually shifted to the annual model change, which whipped up demand even further.

In the mid-1950s, Detroit began a fling with fins. Beginning in 1955, Chevrolet introduced increasingly larger and more drastically-shaped fins on its models. The 1955 Bel-Air had a simple, half-round shape on the quarter panels, with the tail lights imbedded in them. In 1956, that shape was made longer vertically, and the fuel filler door was incorporated in the tail light. One had to turn a piece of the chrome bezel to unlock the door, and then the lamp swung down to reveal the gas cap.

1957 saw the fin morph into a long vertical design, but still not drastically altering the side of the quarter. That began in 1958, with the introduction of a rounded-top fin that caused a significant change in the quarter panel surface. At that time, the fuel filler door was moved to behind the rear license plate.

1959 was the peak year for the fin fling. Chevrolet's fins grew to astronomical proportions, with a huge teardrop rear lamp. After that, it seemed that we had had enough of the fins, and they gradually shrank back into the fenders, becoming more muted, and finally disappeared.

Of course, it wasn't just Chevrolet; all the models of every manufacturer went through a similar metamorphosis. And, they were all similarly creative with the placement of the fuel filler. It was embarrassing to have someone pull in with a brand-new whatever and say 'fill 'er up', and me having no idea where to start. "It's in the left tail lamp!"… "Under the license plate"… "On the other side"… "Behind the bumper"… and on and on.

And, not only that, they couldn't leave the hood latch alone either. Some were in the center, right under the hood leading edge; some were way down below the bumper, or in the middle of the grille. Some were offset to the left, or to the right. It's hard to look professional and competent when you can't find the fuel filler door, or the hood latch.

Willys

Army surplus stores were still a big thing in the '60s. There was one on Route 66 just west of St. Clair where you could buy anything from medic kits to service ribbons and medals to tanks. Yes, tanks! Of course, they had all the armament removed, but still…

Sherman had bought a jeep. It was a real Willys; not new production, but one that had been used by the military somewhere. Of course, it was olive drab, with the white star in a circle on the hood, with a jerry can strapped to the back. Sherman liked to go antelope hunting in Wyoming, and I think his plan was to tow it out there and use it during the hunt. I don't think he ever did though, because he found out that the vehicle wouldn't go over 40 miles per hour without the front wheels going berserk. They would begin to wobble a little at about 40, and unless you slowed down considerably, the wobble would become violent gyrations and almost throw you out of the jeep.

"Hey, Sherman, do you think I could borrow your jeep to take my girl on a picnic?"

Sherman was sitting in the feed store office, smoking one of his trademark 5-cent Phillies. He pulled the cigar out of his mouth blew a couple of his perfect smoke rings. "I don't know. Where are you thinking of going?"

"I thought we could go up to the (Meramec) State Park."

"That's about fifteen miles, and all on the highway. The jeep doesn't do well over 40 miles an hour."

"I'll drive slow, and take it easy. I'll be real careful."

"Okay, as long as you're careful. When do you want to go?"

"Well, I haven't mentioned it to Gail yet, and I'm working nights now, so it would be some morning. I'll have to check with her, but I think day after tomorrow. Will that work?"

"Sure. I was going to wash it today. Maybe you could do that for me."

"You bet!"

"Hey, Gail! How would you like to go on a picnic Friday?"

"Sure! What time?"

"I could pick you up around 10 O'clock. I thought we could drive up to the state park and drive around awhile."

"Ok, sounds like fun."

As I hung up, I was really excited. I was thinking, 'she thinks we are going to ride in the pickup again. Boy will she be surprised to see the jeep!'

And she was. I had the windscreen laying down on the hood, and of course there was no top, and no doors. You could look right down at the pavement just a few inches from where you sat. She got in, and didn't say a lot, except to ask where I had gotten the jeep. We took off down the road, and being the speed freak I was, I immediately pushed the 40 miles-per-hour limit when we got on the highway. First, I noticed the front wheels begin to wobble, and then the whole jeep began to shake and gyrate. Gail was petrified, afraid of being thrown out. Being the extremely sensitive and observant person I am, I had no idea what she was thinking.

"Whoa, I guess we won't go that fast. That was really something, wasn't it?" No answer.

We rode on in silence. When we arrived at the park, and as we were driving around the loop road, I noticed a mound of sand at the side of the road, undoubtedly stored there for road repairs and such. I veered off the road and drove straight into the sand pile, to see if I could get the jeep stuck. As the jeep bogged down in the loose sand, I shifted into four-wheel drive, and the jeep just walked right out of that sand.

"Wow, did you see that? You can't get this thing stuck. Four-wheel drive is fantastic." No answer. Of course, Gail was familiar with being stuck. I think we had been stuck in at least two places before. In fact, I seemed to have a habit of getting into 'sticky' situations. Not long before that, I had pulled over to the side of a gravel road for some petting time, and had slid into a muddy ditch. I had to walk about half a mile to a farmer's house, and ask him to pull me out. In fact, that happened with more than one girl, and on more than one occasion. I can only imagine the mortification of my girl, but at the time, I was completely oblivious.

We drove back to St. Clair without incident, and I dropped Gail off at her house.

"Have any trouble?" Sherman.

"Nope. None. The jeep is really fun, but it's kind of embarrassing to have to drive 40 when everyone else is driving 70 or 80." I didn't mention that I had tried. I thanked him for letting me borrow the jeep, but that was the last time I drove it. Gail wasn't really anxious to do that again, but she never let on.

Rocket 88

Melvin had a 1956 Oldsmobile, with a Rocket 88 engine in it. Olds had created a lot of interest with its introduction of that V8 engine, which had lots of power. Chevrolet had just introduced its first V8 engine in 1955, with its puny 250 cubic-inch version. The next year, Chevy helped that along by boring it out to a 283, which eventually had a very long run as a popular engine, but it could not hold a candle to the Rocket 88.

Normally, Melvin would come roaring into the station at the last minute in a cloud of dust. Today, he came down Old 66, which ran alongside New 66 near the station. The station sat on the outside of the apex of a curve in New 66. There was a slight bluff across the road from the station, so that people coming from the southwest on the new road could not see anyone entering from the old road, from very far off. The same was true of anyone on the old road; one could not see very far down the new road.

Melvin was really late today and as he barreled down old 66, he decided not to stop at the stop sign before crossing the four lanes of

New 66. I mean, what are the chances of actually running into anyone anyhow? Evidently, pretty good.

A car (fortunately, not a truck) smashed into the driver's side of Melvin's Rocket 88 and launched Melvin through the side window. The Olds was thrown onto its side and both cars skidded down the road for several yards before coming to a stop. When Melvin had been thrown out of the car he had been slammed into the road, with his own car forcing him to skid down the concrete pavement along with it. His ear was torn off, and the entire left side of his face was abraded off by the rough concrete. Fortunately, he had not been forced completely under the vehicle, so he had not been crushed.

He was late for work.

Speedy Gonzalez

I didn't have any room to gloat over Melvin's accident. In fact, I felt fortunate nothing like that had happened to me so far. I didn't have a car of my own, as some in my class did. I don't know of anyone whose parents had bought them a car. If they were able to drive a car to school, it was because they had gotten jobs and saved enough to buy it themselves.

There were always vehicles at our house to drive, however. With six kids, and three of them older than me, there was plenty of transportation. Not that a cool teenager would want to drive all of them. My dad had the old seven-ton box truck with the battered beer truck box on it, and the pickup which I already described. It was okay, but second gear had mysteriously quit working, and I had already broken one of the rear springs. Even though I had replaced that myself, it now seemed like damaged goods.

Maxine bought a 1953 mustard yellow (ugly!) Chevrolet, and Janet had a Nash Rambler. Everyone worked, so the cars were in use most of the time. That left the trucks for me (sigh), but if Mom wasn't working, I had access to our 1959 Chevrolet (I already told you how I smashed the beautiful Buick, and that it was replaced with the '59.)

The little six in the 1959 did not have nearly the guts that the Buick had, but I soon discovered that with the manual transmission, so much deception and fun were possible. My recent accident had not taught me any lessons, except that I needed to learn how to drift through curves.

Mom could drive the manual transmission, but she was a terrible driver with it. I think she was terrified of pulling out in traffic, and killing the engine. She would floor the accelerator, causing the engine to scream, and ease out on the clutch. When she got the car rolling about 10 miles per hour, she would shift into second and get completely off the accelerator, so that the car just putted along for a minute, before she then shifted into third.

I was intrigued by the possibilities of down-shifting, up-shifting, double-clutching, coasting in neutral, drifting around curves, etc. I soon discovered that the car would top out at about 95 – uphill or downhill, didn't seem to matter. I drove it so hard that several people thought I had a Corvette engine in it, and were always pestering me to race them. I knew if I took them up on the race, the terrible truth would be out, that I only had a measly six in the car – so, I always demurred, with some lame excuse. Also, I was afraid of dropping a transmission, burning out a clutch or some other disaster that had happened to a few of my friends.

Oermann's bridge sat at the bottom of a hill and crossed the Little Meramec River. The hill was fairly steep, and more than a quarter of a mile long. I decided one evening that I would like to see how fast one would be going at the bottom if one were to begin at the top from a dead stop, in neutral. I drove a little past the top to make sure nobody was coming, turned around and stopped just beyond the crest of the hill.

I left the engine running, shifted into neutral, and took my foot off the brake. It seemed to take forever for the car to even begin rolling, and even then it was not accelerating very much. For a few seconds, I thought this was going to be boring. Then, it began to get a little exciting. I kept my eyes on the speedometer, glancing at the road occasionally. Thirty, 35, 40, 45…now I began watching the road more, and glancing at the speedometer quickly. Now things were happening too quickly. My speed began to pick up more quickly, and the bridge abutments loomed into my vision. Keep the car in the middle of the road. Don't make any sudden adjustments. Should I stop this – no, this is what I came here for and I am going to finish it!

As with most bridges, there was a ramp at the approach to the bridge. To make things more interesting, the bridge did not sit parallel with the line of the road coming down the hill to accommodate a slight curve to the right in the road beyond the bridge. As my car traveled up the approach ramp, it was launched into the air, of course, going whatever direction I was going before leaving earth. The left side bridge railing was getting dangerously close to me as my car thankfully slammed back into the pavement. By this time, I was trying to make the turn to the right, so there was a little skidding involved, but I made it across.

So, how fast was I going at the bottom, the point of the whole stupid exercise? I had no idea. I had been too busy trying desperately not to take a gainer off the bridge in my car.

Most of the county roads back then were gravel. The county would grade out the potholes occasionally, and when they got really bad, would spread new gravel. I still had no good concept of speed control to suit conditions, and drove nearly as fast on those roads as I did on the interstate. It was pretty common for me to get into a twenty- to thirty-degree drift on some curves.

It's one thing for dirt track racers to drift around the racecourse, when the track has been groomed, and the surface is somewhat consistent. However, it is insane to attempt that on gravel roads where there are potholes, and some stretches may have no gravel, while other stretches may contain thick layers of new gravel.

To make matters worse, I didn't just endanger my own life, I drove like that with my girl in the car. We were parked one night in the country, and all of a sudden realized that we were very late starting home. I started down the road at my usual high rate of speed, around 60, in a hurry to get back. At the crest of a hill on this road, there was a very large boulder in the center of the road that was so large, the road crew had just left it in place. Everyone knew about it, and just drove around it. I forgot it was there, and as my headlights revealed it to me, I swerved to avoid smashing into it. That threw the car into a slew that finally put the car perpendicular to the road, and we skidded down to the bottom of the hill (about 80 yards) sideways. We were soooo lucky. The car had not moved off the road into either ditch, which would have likely flipped the car and thrown us out (no seatbelts back then). There was so little room between the ditches that it took me three or four tries going back and forth to get the car straightened out. There was not much talking the rest of the way home. In fact, I can't believe now that she agreed to go out with me again – poor judgement on her part.

In spite of that, I continued to race along all roads at speeds way beyond safe, and for no apparent reason. That was the most spectacular, but not the last time that I spun out on gravel roads. I continued to be blessed in that the car continued to be undamaged, until the last day of high school.

A couple of friends and I, along with our girlfriends, had decided to just go for a ride in the country around St. Clair. I think all of us were newly aware that we would be leaving the area, and that we most likely would never come back, so we wanted to take one last look around. I had driven down Springfield Road west of town, and had pulled up to an intersection and come to a stop (a rare event for me). I looked both ways, but the brush on both sides of the road limited the field of view to only a few yards either way. Just as I pulled into the intersection, an-other car came down the road driving like me (the fool), and T-boned us, smashing the left rear door, and spinning the car completely around. My forward momentum carried me across the intersection, tail fin first. The sideways momentum from the other car drove the rear end of my car about a foot into the clay dirt bank on the far side.

Fortunately, there were no serious injuries.

Not having any cell phones, and being way out in the country, the best alternative was to see if we could drive the car, which we did. After I took everyone home, I drove the car home and told Mom about the wreck. When the insurance adjuster saw the car, and even though it was drivable, he totaled out the car. So, I had totaled two cars in less than two years. And, to make matters worse the other driver had no insurance. Our carrier canceled our insurance. This was a serious financial burden on my parents, since they were already struggling. Now, even though I was getting ready to leave the family and go on to college, they would have to go into assigned risk coverage at a much higher cost. I had really botched their situation with my irresponsibility.

Me and my best girl, Gail, Christmas 1962, at her house

Which Way Did They Go?

I had lots of interests as a teenager, and a lot of academic subjects came easily for me. In music, I played piano and organ for church, but hated to practice. I played clarinet in the concert and marching bands, but didn't see that as resulting in any career chances for me. I played saxophone in the jazz band, but again, didn't see a clear career path in that area. I sang in the high school chorus, boys' glee club and we had our traveling quartet that had achieved some notoriety. I was really interested in music in general, and had given a lot of thought to how I could parlay that into something.

I liked taking care of the livestock we had at home; chickens, cows, horses and miscellaneous pets. I was also experimenting with forestry, in that I had planted a few plum, peach and apple trees from seeds, and had also transplanted some trees. I found that I really liked seeing trees grow into something, each one slightly different. However, I could not see the way to a living. Certainly, Dad's business had hit a wall and my oldest brother Jerry was not having a great time with his efforts in agriculture.

Our class was fortunate in that we had a Shop, or Industrial Arts, class. Mr. Goforth was a great teacher, and I loved the concept of creating things from wood or metal. Maybe I could be a carpenter. However, I did notice that I was awfully slow, so that might not be the best choice either.

One of the new additions to the high school staff was a guidance counselor. He was a kind man, with great intentions, but I did not find him particularly helpful. Not that it was his fault; I was just hoping for some specific direction, and he did not provide it. He pointed out some options for me, which were mostly obvious, but that still left me with several choices. Why couldn't someone just tell me which way to go?

Not that it affected me, but the prejudice against women in industry was in full force then. A lot of my co-ed classmates were advised against careers in science or industry, and pointed to homemaking or secretarial work instead.

Finally, there came a career interest test, and I couldn't wait to see the results so it could point me in the right direction. The results indicated that I should go into music. Unless of course, I wanted to go into science or manufacturing or agriculture, or...(sigh). The guidance counselor said, "You are very lucky. You can do anything you want to do." Great. But, how to make a choice.

Maxine, my oldest sister, had recently married Bob, who had taken an active interest in me. We had several conversations about career choices, and he helped me to see the advantages and disadvantages of each one. He was on his way to becoming an electrical engineer so his advice was naturally slanted in that direction, but I also think he was fair and somewhat balanced in his thought process. In the end, he had caused me to give more consideration to engineering.

Another factor that weighed heavily in my decision was the space race that was heating up just then. Because of the Soviet Union's success in launching Sputnik and then other satellites, President Kennedy challenged the US to set a goal of putting a man on the moon within a decade. There was a considerable shortage of engineers at that time already, and the president's challenge caused a prediction of a shortage in engineers amounting to hundreds of thousands. Engineering seemed to be the place to be, and several of my friends were thinking of the same thing.

Glenn, Fred and I were in the same economic boat. None of us could attend college without some additional funding, and none of our parents were in any position to help. I applied for a Pell Grant, and was granted a very small amount of assistance from that. Also, in spite of my lackluster performance academically, I was recognized as a National Merit Scholar, but there was no money attached to that.

Glenn and I decided to investigate Missouri School of Mines in Rolla. Rolla is a land grant college, and recognized as one of the best undergraduate engineering schools in the country. Even better, it was very close to home, being only fifty miles away. We found that we could join one of many supper clubs at the school, where one could get several meals each week at a very reasonable cost, in return for working at the club washing dishes or serving tables several times each week.

Fred, Gary, and others in our class considered going into engineering with schooling at Rolla as well, so for a while it appeared that our class would have lots of engineers. Life has a way of getting in the way of the best-laid plans however, and as it turned out, none of us went to Rolla, at least right away. Gary and Glenn decided to go into liberal arts, and went to Southwest Missouri State in Springfield. Fred went into the Air Force, primarily due to financial considerations. I was left as the only one headed directly into engineering, and planning to go to Rolla by myself.

Then, a rare opportunity came our way. The University of Chicago offered full scholarships to several small high schools in the Midwest, and St. Clair High received one of them. It was left to school administration to choose to whom it should be awarded. The decision was made to use the SAT score as the award criterion. Since the test was not offered at that time anywhere close to us, three of us were chosen to drive to Rolla, fifty miles away, to take the test. Gloria, Gerard and I were chosen for that opportunity, even though I wasn't in the top ten percent of the class, and we drove there on a Saturday morning. The final award date arrived before the test results came back, so the school had to make a choice without the test results. Gerard got the nod, and so received the full scholarship to a wonderful engineering school.

Bob and Maxine were married, and he obtained a position with the Guide Lamp Division of General Motors, in Anderson, Indiana, as an electrical engineer in the Electronics Laboratory. He continued to look out for me, and we would talk about careers whenever they came to visit. During one of those visits, he told me that General Motors had an engineering school called General Motors Institute (GMI), that operated as a work-study arrangement. One had to be accepted by both the school and a participating division, which would support the student by paying an hourly wage for time worked.

I read the brochures he gave me, and initially did not care for the idea. It didn't really seem like going to college to me, and I didn't like the idea that it took five years to complete, since half of every year was given to work. However, as things were developing none of my friends would be going to Rolla with me anyway, and after working on budgets for some time, it became apparent that it would take me at least five years to complete a four-year degree there also, because I couldn't make enough money working summers and extra jobs at the school to continue without a work break to save more.

GMI began to look better the more I looked at it. I was assured to learn that the school was fully accredited as an undergraduate engineering school. I would have a secure job to earn money for tuition and books, and Bob had graciously offered that I could live with them during work sessions, so I wouldn't have to pay rent for half the year.

I had applied at Rolla previously, and received notice that I had been accepted there. However, it was becoming increasingly obvious that Rolla was not a very viable option for me. The discouraging things (for me) about the GMI entrance requirements were that students were to be in the top ten percent of their high school graduating class, and were required to have more science and math classes than I had taken. I had taken all the math and science that our school offered, but the school did not offer a second semester of calculus, or some of the other advanced biology, physics, etc., classes that GMI wanted.

I had little hope that I could be accepted by the school, but with

Bob's encouragement, I applied anyway. As far as a plant, I just chose to apply to the place where Bob worked, since he had said I could stay with them. I could have chosen the Corvette assembly plant, or one of the other plants in the St. Louis area, but frankly I did not even think of those. It seemed to me that I had but one path to college. In the end, I was glad that I had chosen Guide Lamp, for a lot of reasons, but that is another story.

About a week before graduation, I received notice that I had been accepted by both GMI and Guide Lamp! How in the world had that happened? I discovered much later that Guide Lamp had decided to sponsor five students for the 1963 incoming class, and I was not in the initial five. One of the five that had been selected decided to attend somewhere else however, and the student coordinator, Buck Rice, had said, "Hey, what about that chicken farmer from Missouri?" Nobody had any other suggestions, so I became part of the Freshman class of 1963 at GMI. Once again, luck had played a significant part in directing my future path.

Next Chapter

The fleet was steaming into harm's way. The battleship Missouri was accompanied by several destroyers and the carrier Enterprise, as Mustangs, Thunderbolts and Corsairs flew air cover. Suddenly, the fleet was under attack! Rounds began crashing into the hulls of the destroyers, then the Missouri. The planes flying cover were being decimated by some unknown force.

I was daydreaming. During my elementary and middle school years, I had assembled several plastic models of military vehicles of all sorts, and had displayed them in my bedroom. The planes had been hung from the ceiling with string fastened to the ceiling with thumbtacks, and strung under the wings. The ships, tanks and trucks had been displayed around the room on windowsills, the dresser and chest of drawers.

Today, I was leaving for college. I knew I would never be back.

At least, not back to stay. It was time for me to begin writing the next chapter in my life. As the Bible says, it was time for me to '…put away childish things…'. Although I still loved to look at the models, there was no way for me to take them with me, and I couldn't expect my parents to keep them around. I had gathered them up and taken them outside to one of my favorite places; the play house out back. I arranged them around the plum tree that I had planted a couple of years before, and began shooting them up with my air rifle.

As I had decimated the fleet, I sat there thinking about recent events and what was coming next. Events of the month before graduation had seemed like a tornado tearing through our class, ripping us apart, tearing us into individual pieces of chaff. Some had already made marriage plans while others had enlisted or been drafted into the military, and were headed off to Vietnam. What had been, just a few weeks ago, a gang of four or five that was going to descend on Rolla School of Mines and take over the engineering world, had disappeared into none of us going there. We had talked of how we would room together, take the same classes, study together, and perhaps end up working for the same company, or at least close to each other. Maybe we would all work for the rapidly expanding space program and help the US to challenge the Russians by assisting with our own rocket development efforts.

That was all gone. I had no idea what General Motors Institute would be like. I did know though, that I had to leave my steady girlfriend Gail, and I was very anxious about not being able to see her. During high school we had been inseparable. I walked her to school every morning. During my Senior year, we had dated at least four times every week. When I had run errands for my father and brother, I had picked her up and she had ridden with me as I delivered feed or picked up eggs from farmers. We had been in the band together. Now, weeks would go by before I would be able to see her. Would she stand by me, or find someone else?

Had I made the right decision about my education and career? Would I really be any good as an engineer? And, how about working in a factory. I had no idea how that would be. I reflected on the role that both good and not-so-good people had played in my life so far.

On balance, the influence of the church I attended had been very positive. The good people there had looked after me and guided me both by example and verbal instruction. I believe to this day that my life might not have been as good as it has without their influence, love and guidance. By the same token, most of the people in town had shown me good intentions and support in many ways. From my dad and the rest of my family, I had inherited a strong work ethic which would sustain me initially through the struggle to finish a college curriculum in competition with mostly high school valedictorians, and then later in the industrial workforce.

Perversely, even the not-so-good people had helped me find my way. Because of the strong mores that had been instilled in me by family, church, townsfolks and friends, I could see that I wanted to be known as an honest, caring and hardworking person, not someone who would cheat his own mother, or be lazy at work.

I had packed all my worldly goods into two new suitcases that Mom had bought for me, including my new Kueffel & Esser, Log Log Duplex Decitrig slide rule (in a scabbard with a handy belt loop) that I would need for engineering school, and was waiting for Gail's parents to come by and drive me to Anderson, Indiana to begin my new life.

I was concerned about my relationship with Gail. I still didn't own a car, and how would we remain together, with me 300 miles away? Would she remain true to me, or would she find someone else? For that matter, could I remain true to her, or would I find someone else? For the last two years, we had never been separated for more than a day at a time. Should we just break it off now, and avoid the misery later? No, I loved her too much. How could I even think of that? How could we ever see each other again? Gail's parents certainly couldn't drive her to see me every week, and I didn't want her to drive that far by herself, even if her parents would let her. Then there was the fact that for six months of every year, I would be even farther away, in Flint, Michigan, going to school.

Then there was that – how was I going to compete with a class that was made up of mostly Valedictorians and Salutatorians, from much larger schools, and with lots more math and science under their belts than I had? How would I ever catch up? If I were honest with myself,

I would have to admit that I was scared to death of failure for the first time in my life, of letting down my parents, Bob and Maxine, and Gail. Embarrassment would consume me if I didn't make it at GMI – and, then what would I do?

In thinking over my life to that point, I knew that I had done some things well, and some not so well. My biggest disappointment with myself to date had been that I continued working in a situation that I did not think was right. Yes, I had resisted the worst of the practices, but was tarred with the same brush by being there. I would have to work out what to do as I met similar situations in the future. One thing I had settled on. I would try to live my life in accordance with my watchword: Integrity. I would be honest, give my best effort, and try to understand others' needs and feelings. My worries and concerns all came down to one question. Would the rest of my life be…

Regular or Ethyl?